HOW TO DO just about ANYTHING

Computer Essentials

READER'S DIGEST

HOW TO DO just about ANYTHING
Computer Essentials

Published by The Reader's Digest Association Limited
London • New York • Sydney • Montreal

Contents

Windows Vista

Word

Excel

How to use this book

Windows, Word and Excel are three of the most important pieces of software that you can have on your computer. The clear instructions in this book guide you through the basic features of each program, with step-by-step projects and accompanying pictures showing you exactly what you will see on screen and helpful tips to save you time and effort.

GETTING AROUND THE BOOK

Split into three clear and informative sections, this easy-to-use guide will get you started with Windows Vista, Word and Excel.

WINDOWS VISTA

By mastering the key aspects of the Windows operating system, you will soon be able to move easily around your computer system, adapt the settings to suit your particular needs and keep your computer in good working order. The projects included in this book will give you all the help you require in order to arrange a window, move files and folders, create keyboard shortcuts, maximise available disk space and deal effectively with any computer viruses.

WORD

Once you know how to use this word-processing program effectively, you will be able to undertake a range of useful tasks with your computer. Follow the projects to learn how to enter text into a document, pick the right font, format your text, delete, add and move words, use Autocorrect, add a picture and print your documents.

EXCEL

Find out how creating spreadsheets and sorting information can help to unclutter your life. This book shows you how to save your work, add columns, rows and page breaks to spreadsheets, use AutoSum calculations, style, align and sort data and print your work.

WHICH VERSION?

This book assumes that you're using a PC with Windows Vista Home Premium edition installed on it. It also provides information based on a PC using Microsoft Office Word 2007 and Microsoft Excel 2007 (both part of Office 2007 Small Business edition).

The snapshots images of Windows Vista are as it looks after being newly installed, with four Desktop icons added. If the windows and folders look different from those on your screen, don't worry; the features and tools are very similar or even identical.

If you have an earlier version of Word or Excel on your computer, you'll find that it looks different, but the functions are very similar or even identical. You can upgrade your PC from an earlier version of Office or if Word and Excel are new to you, you can install the Office suite from scratch.

Close up
These project-related tips offer you extra detail on software functions.

Bright idea
Wondering how to use your new-found skills? Look out for these tips.

Key word
You'll find handy definitions of technical words or phrases here.

GETTING AROUND THE PAGE

Illustrated steps and a range of visual features guide you through the tasks in this book. Here are the key items you should look for on each page.

Before you start

Projects begin with a small section of text. This outlines important points to consider and anything you need to do before beginning the project.

Snapshots

Pictures of the PC screen – 'snapshots' – show you what you'll see on your own screen at each stage of the project.

Enclosed sections

Menus, buttons or key sections of the screen are highlighted so you can locate them easily.

Bold type

Any bold text is a command for you to carry out. You may need to select a menu option, a toolbar button or press a key.

See also

These are cross references to other pages containing related information.

Features

A topic is sometimes presented as a feature, giving lots of general advice and tips, rather than explaining a specific task in a step-by-step format. Often, annotated images will illustrate items of particular importance.

Step-by-step

Projects are set out in easy-to-follow steps with accompanying snapshots.

Useful tips

Find explanations of the more complex aspects of a task and alternative ways to do things.

Page turns

The arrow in the bottom right corner of a page indicates that the project continues over the page.

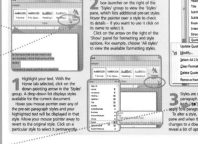

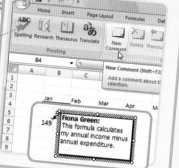

Add a comment

To insert a comment, first select the cell to which you want to attach the comment, then click on the **Review** tab and then on **New Comment** in the 'Comments' group. A small window pops up, into which you can enter some explanatory text. Click away from the comment when you have finished typing. A red triangle is displayed in the top right of the cell indicating there is a comment attached.

That's amazing!
You can enhance the way you work on a PC using these inspiring ideas, explanations and items of special interest.

Watch out
These tips warn you of possible difficulties and pitfalls you may encounter, and give helpful advice on how to avoid problems.

Expert advice
Advanced tips offer guidance on specific features and useful advice on how to achieve professional results.

Set up your PC safely

When you are choosing a suitable location for your PC, check that there is enough space for all the equipment and an adequate number of mains outlets. You also need to consider lighting and seating, and the surface area of your desk. If you want to connect to the Internet, you will also need to be near a telephone socket unless you have a wireless connection.

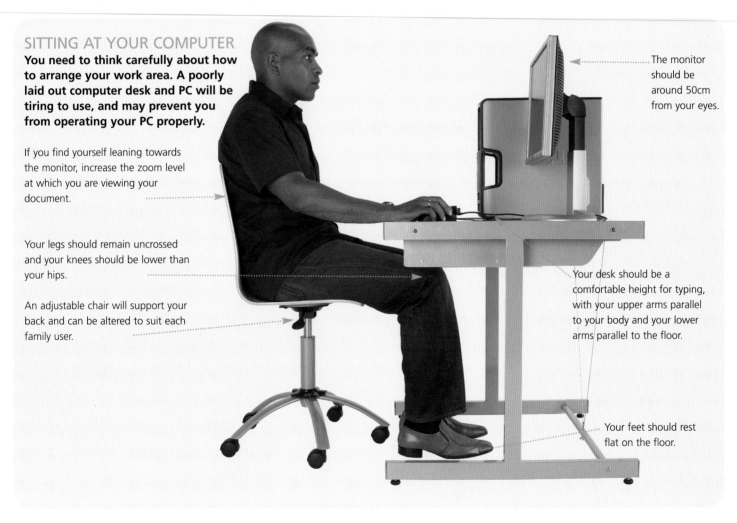

SITTING AT YOUR COMPUTER

You need to think carefully about how to arrange your work area. A poorly laid out computer desk and PC will be tiring to use, and may prevent you from operating your PC properly.

If you find yourself leaning towards the monitor, increase the zoom level at which you are viewing your document.

Your legs should remain uncrossed and your knees should be lower than your hips.

An adjustable chair will support your back and can be altered to suit each family user.

The monitor should be around 50cm from your eyes.

Your desk should be a comfortable height for typing, with your upper arms parallel to your body and your lower arms parallel to the floor.

Your feet should rest flat on the floor.

NAMING AND PLACING PARTS

Your PC's hardware includes all the parts that you can actually see and handle. Knowing how to position these elements ensures a safe and efficient work area.

System unit
This is the part of your computer to which everything is connected. Leave space so that you can plug in the cables easily and to allow for ventilation. Don't leave cables trailing.

Monitor
This is the computer's screen. Position your monitor to avoid reflections, but do not face a bright window yourself as this may lead to eyestrain.

Speakers
For the best sound quality, speakers should be placed on either side of the monitor and at desk level or higher, not just pushed under the desk.

Printer
Position your printer near the system unit. Make sure there is sufficient space around it for loading the paper trays.

Keyboard
Make sure the keyboard is on a stable and level surface within easy reach. Leave enough space in front of it for hands and wrists. Ensure that the desk is at the correct height.

Mouse
Place the mouse to the side of your keyboard that suits whether you are left or right-handed. Use a mouse mat to create the correct amount of friction, and be sure there is plenty of room to move the mouse around.

Expert advice
If you are planning to use your computer for long periods, either surfing the Internet or preparing your accounts and letters, then you should invest in a good-quality comfortable office chair. Most dining chairs do not offer the support for your back that is vitally important when you are sitting still for long periods. Also, most office chairs are adjustable and so will suit every member of the family. Remember, even with a comfortable chair, you should take regular 10 minute breaks to walk around.

What is Windows?

Your computer uses a piece of software called an 'operating system' in order to run programs and control its hardware. The system used on most PCs is Windows. It provides the connection between the user and the software, and allows the PC to perform tasks, such as printing. Windows Vista, the most recent version of Windows, is fast, reliable, and very easy to use.

SEE ALSO...
- *What you see first* p20
- *Moving around a window* p22

WINDOWS

Using Windows is not as difficult as it may seem. The general principles of working with an operating system are easy to learn, and you'll be surprised at how often the same processes crop up, even in different **programs**. In fact, Windows is designed this way – if you know how to open and save a file in one program, you will be able to do it in all Windows programs.

Operating system

The term 'operating system' refers to software that enables the computer's hardware to 'talk' to its programs and its users. While people communicate with words, the computer uses a digital language of electrical 'on' and 'off' pulses.

The operating system translates your key presses, mouse movements and clicks into a binary language of 1s (on) and 0s (off), which the PC's processor can understand and manipulate. Once the task is finished, the results are translated back into a form we can read on the screen.

Quick Desktop tour

If you bought a computer with Windows Vista pre-installed, you may only be able to see the Recycle Bin on your Desktop. However, you can add icons for quick access to other areas of your PC, the Internet and any other computers linked to yours. To do this, right-click on a blank area of the Desktop and choose **Personalize**. Click on **Change desktop icons** from the 'Tasks' pane on the left and, in the Desktop Icon Settings dialogue box that appears, put ticks next to 'Computer', 'User's Files', 'Network', and 'Control Panel'. Then click on **OK**.

Icons can represent physical components, such as your hard disk or a printer, or virtual locations on your hard disk, such as the Recycle Bin or the Documents folder. When you install a new program, a shortcut icon may appear on your Desktop, usually with a small, dark arrow in the corner. To access the program, place the mouse pointer over the icon and double-click.

Start menu

The Start menu contains shortcuts to your PC's software. Click on the **Start** button, then on **All Programs** and you'll see a list of applications. Just click on one, and the program opens. The Start menu enables you to quickly access recently used documents and the programs you use most often. From here, you can also adjust your PC's settings, search for files, browse the Internet and look for help on a variety of topics.

Dialogue boxes

Sometimes Windows and its programs need instructions. When this happens, you use an on-screen dialogue box to make choices – the box may pop up and ask you to confirm or alter an action or it may appear after you click on a menu item or button, offering a range of options to tick or select. One of the most common dialogue boxes appears when you close a file. If you haven't saved since you last made changes to that file, the dialogue box will give you the option to save it before closing.

Key word
A program is software designed to allow the user to carry out a specific task, such as writing a letter or calculating a bank balance. To see which programs are on your PC, click on the Start *button and then on* All Programs.

Every program or file you open is viewed on screen in a 'window' on the surrounding Desktop. Your Desktop may look slightly different from the one shown here, depending on whether you upgraded to Vista or bought a PC with it pre-installed.

Recycle Bin This is where your deleted files are stored, ready for final removal.

Computer Easy access to files and folders in the various drives on your PC.

Title bar Dark when active, light when inactive, this often shows the window's name and icon.

Minimize, Maximize and Restore Minimize (left) reduces a window to a button on the Taskbar. Maximize (centre) expands a window to fill the Desktop; click on this button again to restore a window to its original size. **Close** (right), when red, shuts a window or program.

User folder Double-click on this icon to open the User window.

User name Displays the user who is currently logged onto your PC.

Frequently used programs The programs you use most often are listed here.

Control Panel Allows you to change your computer's settings.

All Programs Gives you access to all the programs on your PC.

Start button Click here and navigate pop-up menus to access most items on your PC.

Quick Launch bar An area where you can put shortcuts to favourite programs.

Search box Type in a file name to search for a lost file on your computer.

Address bar Shows where you are and gives you access to other drives on your PC and Web locations.

Menu bar Lists the series of drop-down menus containing commands.

Windows Sidebar Displays small programs called gadgets, such as a clock, slide show and news feed headlines.

Notification area Change date and time, and set the volume level here.

Program and window buttons The active program button is black. Other programs and minimised windows are grey. Click once to select an item.

Taskbar Contains the **Start** button and useful shortcuts.

Expert advice
If you can't see the Quick Launch Toolbar, right-click on the **Taskbar** and select **Toolbars** followed by **Quick Launch**. A row of icons will appear just to the right of the Start button (see above). You can add your own shortcuts to this area by clicking and dragging. If there isn't room for new icons, right-click on the **Taskbar** and click on **Lock the Taskbar** to remove the tick. Then drag the vertical dotted line to the right. Finally, right-click on the **Taskbar** and select **Lock the Taskbar** again.

Close up
When you double-click on a document to open it, the program in which it was created should open automatically. This means you do not need to open the program separately before you can access the document.

THE WORLD OF WINDOWS

The Windows operating system has been updated many times since it was introduced in 1983. It is now capable of performing a wide array of tasks.

A brief history

The original Microsoft operating system was called MS-DOS (Microsoft – Disk Operating System). To instruct the computer to carry out an action, you typed your commands into a text-only screen. It was successful and reliable but not particularly easy to use, as you had to learn complex instructions for individual actions.

Windows 3.1, released in 1992, used a 'GUI' (Graphical User Interface), which featured simple screen icons and windows. You could point, click on and drag and drop icons with a mouse to give your PC instructions.

The next major upgrades to the system were Windows 95, Windows 98, Me and XP. The most recent version is Windows Vista, which features a new user interface and exciting multimedia features. This new 'look and feel' combines with greater reliability and speed to create the whole Vista experience.

Keep up to date

The Microsoft Corporation work continually on their software to fix problems, or 'bugs', which arise with new versions, and to improve Windows' performance. You can download the latest updates to your current operating system free of charge from the Internet. Just click on

the **Start** button and select **All programs**, followed by **Windows Update**. This starts your Internet browser program and, once you're connected to the Internet, accesses Microsoft's Web site for information and downloads.

Help and Support

Windows has a useful Help system as well as Troubleshooting features to answer questions, guide you through tasks and help you to solve problems (see page 89). The Help menu, on the right of the Menu bar, offers options relevant to the current program. Help may also appear as a small '?' button on the far right of a window's Title bar. If you click on this, a '?' symbol appears, which stays with the

mouse pointer. When you click on an item or command on which you need help, an information box will be displayed.

To open the Help and Support Center, click on the **Start** button and select **Help and Support** from the panel on the right. This displays help

categories and topics, and provides links to the Internet for further help. Certain tasks have 'Wizards' associated with

them, which offer step-by-step instructions in dialogue boxes to guide you through the specific task. Troubleshooting Wizards diagnose and solve technical problems, and can be accessed via Help and Support.

Programs galore

Your PC comes with a variety of programs already installed. There is a basic text editing program called Notepad and a word processor called WordPad. There is also an Address Book, a Calculator and a graphics package called Paint.

Your entire digital library – music, photos, videos and TV – can be found in the Windows Media Center. The Media Player can play CDs and **MP3** files as well as most video formats. You can also listen to your favourite radio station through your computer's speakers using Media Player's Internet Radio Station Finder.

Windows DVD Maker and Windows Movie Maker enable you to import, edit and save your home movies on your computer. If you use a digital camera, transferring your images onto your computer's hard disk is also easier than ever as Windows Vista helps you copy your pictures from a digital camera or a scanner.

Key word
MP3 is short for 'MPEG audio Layer-3'. The term names both the technology involved and the format for compressing audio files. MP3 files are much smaller than the original audio files, yet the sound quality remains high. MP3 files are ideal for use on portable music players and on the Internet.

Watch out
Make sure you buy the correct version of Windows Vista. There is an upgrade from Windows XP or a full version for people who can't upgrade, for example, those with Windows 95 or 98. It is easy to upgrade or install – just put the CD-ROM in your disc drive, and the setup software will do everything else for you. If you are upgrading, you will need your previous Windows CD-ROM.

What is Word?

Word processors are programs that enable you to create, save and print documents. Once you have created a document, you can re-use it as often as you like, making any changes and corrections you wish. Word is one of the most versatile word processors available. It makes editing and styling your documents quick, easy and fun.

SEE ALSO...
- *Explore the program p54*
- *Entering text p58*
- *Style and colour text p64*

WHAT YOU CAN DO

Word offers you an impressive range of options to help make your documents look good and save you time.

Choose from a wide range of typefaces, known as 'fonts', which you can set in different sizes, styles – such as bold, italic or underline – and colours. You can even use special effects, so the text sparkles or flashes, for example.

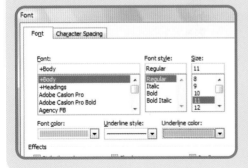

Design your page

You can set your document to the page size that suits you, choose the size of the margins, how text is aligned, and whether you want it in columns. You can insert boxes and tables, set paragraph indents, and add bullet points or automatically number lists. If you want to illustrate your text, there is a huge library of ClipArt available, or you can insert your own illustrations and photographs.

Work faster with templates

If you're not so keen on setting up documents from scratch, try using Word's ready-made templates instead. These include letterheads, memos, faxes and brochure templates.

Word perfect

Word's Spelling and Grammar facility alerts you to misspelt words and badly constructed sentences. If you're stuck for an alternative word, try using the Thesaurus.

Saving time

If you need to do a mail shot, the Mail Merge facility is the perfect tool to use. Create your letter with gaps left for information, such as names and addresses. Then, using Word's step-by-step guide, merge the letter with data records that have been created in Word or ones that have been imported from a database.

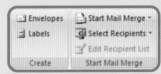

Word and the Office suite

Although you can buy Word 2007 as a separate program, it usually comes as one of a suite of programs, collectively named 'Microsoft Office'. The software programs bundled in Office vary, depending on which version you buy. The version used in this publication – 'Microsoft Office Small Business Edition' – includes Excel, a spreadsheet program, PowerPoint for creating on-screen presentations with sound and animation, and Outlook, an information management program that also allows you to send and receive e-mails.

GETTING AROUND IN WORD

If this is your first time using a word processing program, you'll need a few tips to get you started.

Using the mouse

You use the mouse to point at different areas of the screen and to issue commands. It is designed to sit comfortably under your hand, with your index finger poised over the left button. You will mostly click with the left button, but sometimes you'll need to use the right. When you are following the instructions in this book, 'clicking' the mouse refers to the left button. If you need to use the right, you'll be told to 'right-click'.

When you move the mouse over text on screen, it changes from a white selection arrow

to the insertion point, which looks like a capital I (see left). If you want to enter text, click the insertion point where you want it and type. To select a button on a toolbar or a menu at the top of the screen, point the selection arrow and click.

Double-clicking the left mouse button is a speedy way to select and confirm an option.

Selecting text

To select a whole line of text, position the arrow over the white area on the left of your document,

next to your chosen line, and click once. It will be highlighted instantly. To select more, or less, than one line, click in front of the first character and, with the button held down, drag the mouse over the text as far up, down, left or right as you require. Release the button when you have selected all the text you want. This is known as 'click and drag'.

To select just one word, double-click on it with your left mouse button. If you click three times, you select the whole paragraph. Once you have

selected an area of text, you can style it, change font or font size, copy and paste it into another part of the document, or delete it.

Moving around the page

You can scroll through your document by clicking on the arrows at either end of the scroll bars to the right and along the bottom of the screen, or by dragging the grey block on the scroll bar up or down.

Ribbon button commands

Near the top of the screen, below the window title, is the Ribbon. This gives you immediate access to a wide range of useful controls. Hover your mouse pointer over a button icon to display a pop-up window showing the command that button performs. Some buttons, like 'Paste', for

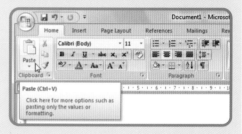

example, display a drop-down menu when you click on the button. Additionally, if applicable, the keyboard short-cut that can be used to perform the action is displayed (see list overleaf).

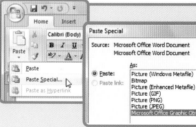

Close up
Using Word 2007, you can open a document that has been created in an older version of Word. However, you cannot use an older version of Word to open a document created in Word 2007.

USING THE KEYBOARD

Function keys are shortcuts to commands:
F1 accesses Microsoft Help and Support.
F2 is for moving text. Select your text, press **F2**, click the point on your page where you wish the text to go to and press the **Return** key.
F4 repeats your last command.

F5 opens a dialogue box for 'Find' and 'Replace' features, and 'Go To', which enables you to jump to another part of your document.
F7 checks a document for spelling and grammar.
F12 Creates a duplicate version of your document using the 'Save As' feature.

Insert allows you to type over existing text.
Delete gets rid of any selected text or item.
Home places the cursor at the start of the line.
End places the cursor at the end of the line.
Page Up places the cursor at the top of the page.
Page Down places the cursor at the page bottom.

Caps Lock causes all the letters that you type to appear as capitals.
Shift allows you to type a letter on a key as a capital or to select the topmarked option on the key. For example, pressing 'Shift' + '5' types the '%' symbol.
Ctrl and **Alt** keys, when pressed in conjunction with other keys, access different commands (keyboard shortcuts). For example, 'Ctrl' + 'P' displays the Print dialogue box.
Ctrl + Alt + Delete is a useful way to quit Word, should your screen freeze up.
Windows key Accesses the Start menu.

Spacebar adds spaces between words.

Return creates a paragraph break or ends a line early.

Backspace deletes text to the left of your cursor.

Arrow keys move the cursor up, down, left and right.

Enter key works like the Return key.

Keyboard shortcuts

You can use all kinds of shortcuts to style your text, format your pages and access commands.

Ctrl + Shift + Spacebar creates a non-breaking space. This means that the words either side of the space are kept together on the same line.
Ctrl + Shift + hyphen creates a non-breaking hyphen. This means that a hyphenated word will not be split over two lines.
Ctrl + Q removes paragraph formatting.
Ctrl + Spacebar removes character formatting.
Ctrl + B makes text bold.
Ctrl + U underlines text.
Ctrl + I italicises text.
Ctrl + Shift + < decreases font size.
Ctrl + Shift + > increases font size.
Ctrl + F2 previews how your page will look when it is printed.
Ctrl + F4 closes the window you're working in.
Ctrl + F6 goes to the next open Word window.
Alt + F4 closes the Word program.
Alt + F8 runs a pre-recorded macro.
Alt + F10 maximises the Word window.

Close up
Use the Help menu to find out more about Word's function keys and shortcuts using Alt and Ctrl. Click the question mark icon on the right of the Ribbon and type in 'keyboard shortcuts'. Click Search.

What is Excel?

Excel is a program that creates spreadsheets. A spreadsheet consists of a grid of cells, arranged in columns and rows, which can contain numbers, formulas or text. You can use spreadsheets to do almost anything, from calculating and analysing your personal and business accounts, to logically storing and sorting lists of addresses or everyday items.

Close up
Excel calls its spreadsheets 'worksheets'. An Excel file is called a workbook and can contain multiple worksheets, accessed by clicking tabs at the bottom of the screen.

WHAT YOU CAN DO

An Excel spreadsheet enables you to organise numerical data, to perform calculations and to present the results in a logical and clear format. As well as calculating values, you can also use Excel to manage lists of information.

Perform calculations

Excel is a powerful calculating tool – once you've entered your data, you can create formulas to instruct the spreadsheet to take the values from specified cells, perform a calculation and then display the answer. Excel contains hundreds of built-in formulas, called functions, which can help you do anything from totalling a column of figures to analysing a company's staff costs over a five-year period. Even the most sophisticated Excel spreadsheets use the basic mathematical operators – plus, minus, multiply, divide and equals – to perform their calculations.

A3	▼		f_x	=A1+A2
	A	B	C	D
1	2			
2	3			
3	5			
4				

Store your data

Excel can handle text as well as numbers, and is an excellent means of storing and organising information, such as a list of club members or an inventory of your home contents. It has lots of useful features to help you enter and view your data quickly and easily, and to present the information in a clear, informative way. You can sort lists alphabetically, filter the contents of a list so that only certain items are visible, or even use Excel's built-in functions (see left) to automatically count how many items in a list match the specified criteria.

Choose a style

Once you have entered your data, it makes sense to style your column and row headings as well as the results of the calculations so that they stand out. Excel includes familiar tools that are common to the Microsoft Office Suite of programs, such as fonts (typefaces), styles, colours and borders. You can even format each cell individually to draw the reader's eye to important items.

Design your page

Like a word processor document, spreadsheets can be formatted to suit your particular needs. There are options to align text, add headers and footers and modify page shape and size. And

there's also a useful feature to make sure all the selected information fits onto the page. Excel has access to the Office Clip Art resources and you can add pictures and WordArt to spreadsheets to illustrate your information and add interest to your spreadsheet. If you would like to display your data in a pictorial form, you can choose from a range of colourful two and three-dimensional graphs.

On-line support

If you need help with using Excel, press **F1** on the keyboard to open the Excel Help window. If you have an on-line connection to the Internet you will see an indicator at the bottom right of the window. This means you can search the Internet for the latest information on all Excel topics.

The Task Pane

This is a special pane that appears at the right-hand side of Excel's window when you want to insert Clip Art into a spreadsheet. To view this pane, click on the **Insert** tab on the Ribbon and then on **Clip Art** in the 'Illustrations' group. The pane allows you to search for Clip Art, photos or movies on your computer or on-line.

THE SPREADSHEET WINDOW

When you launch Excel it automatically displays 'Sheet 1' of a new blank workbook called 'Book 1' in the Excel window. By default, Excel offers three blank worksheets within a workbook.

Quick Access Toolbar
A customisable toolbar of one-click buttons to activate common commands.

Office Button
Gives access to options for opening, printing and saving documents, and lists recently opened documents.

Tabs
Click on a tab on the Ribbon to access a range of related commands.

Group name
Buttons for similar commands are organised in groups on the Ribbon.

Name box
The co-ordinates (column letter and row number) of the selected cell are indicated here. You can use this box to name sections of your sheet for easier navigation and printing.

Selected cell
A black border indicates the selected cell.

Row headers
These numbers identify each row. Using a combination of a column letter and a row number, each cell is given a unique address.

Worksheet tabs
These tabs allow the user to switch between worksheets. Right-click on a tab to insert, remove, rename or move worksheets.

Windows Taskbar
Contains the Start button and some useful shortcuts to your programs and settings.

Column headers
Each column is identified by a letter, or letters.

Mouse pointer
When the mouse pointer becomes a cross, you can select cells or drag items.

Formula Bar
The contents of the selected cell are displayed here for editing.

Close buttons
The red button with a white cross closes Excel.

Maximize/Restore Down button
If this button displays a square, clicking on it will enlarge the Excel window so it fills the screen. If the button contains two overlapping squares, clicking on it will shrink the window.

Minimize button
Click here to reduce the Excel window to a button on the Taskbar. Click on this button to restore the window.

Scroll bars
Use the arrows to move slowly around the spreadsheet. Drag the scroll boxes to move quickly up and down or from left to right.

Task Pane
This displays search options, results and quick links to Clip Art held on your PC and available on-line.

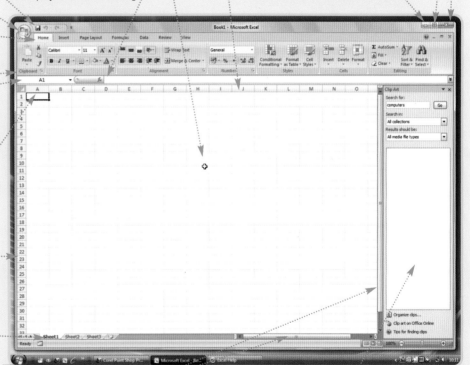

USING THE KEYBOARD

Function keys are shortcuts to commands:
F1 accesses **Microsoft Help and Support**.
F2 is for editing data either in a cell or on the **Formula Bar**: select a cell and press **F2**, use the mouse or arrow keys to position the insertion point and then edit the cell's contents.

F4 repeats your last command.
F5 opens a Go To dialogue box, which enables you to jump to another part of your document.
F7 checks a document for spelling.
F11 inserts a chart using the selected data.
F12 opens the Save As dialogue box.

Delete gets rid of any selected data or item.
Home takes you to column A.
End plus any arrow key moves in the selected direction to the last cell in your data range.
Page Up moves up one screen at a time.
Page Down moves down one screen at a time.

Tab moves you one cell to the right.
Caps Lock makes all the letters that you type appear as capitals.
Shift allows you to type a letter as a capital or to select the top-marked option on a key. For example, pressing **Shift + 5** types the **%** symbol.
Ctrl and **Alt** keys, when pressed separately in conjunction with other keys, provide quick access to certain commands. For example, **Ctrl + P** displays the Print dialogue box.
Windows key accesses the **Start** menu.

Spacebar adds spaces between words.
Return key confirms any data you have entered in a cell.
Backspace deletes text to the left of your cursor.

Arrow (cursor) keys navigate up, down, left and right to adjacent cells.

Enter key works like the **Return** key.

Keyboard shortcuts

You can use all kinds of shortcuts to style your data and format your spreadsheets:

Ctrl + Home moves you to cell A1.
Ctrl + B makes data in the selected cell(s) bold.
Ctrl + U underlines data.
Ctrl + I italicises data.
Ctrl + A selects the entire spreadsheet.
Ctrl + Z undoes the last action.
Ctrl + Y repeats the last action.
Ctrl + Spacebar selects the entire column.

Shift + Spacebar selects the entire row.
Shift + F5 displays the Find dialogue box.
Shift + F2 edits a comment.
Shift + Tab confirms a cell entry and moves one cell to the left.

Alt + F4 closes the Excel program.
Alt + F8 runs a pre-recorded macro.
Alt + Return starts a new line in a cell.

Close up
Use the Help *feature to find out more about Excel's function keys and shortcuts using* Alt *and* Ctrl. *Click the question mark icon on the far right of the window above the Ribbon. Type in 'keyboard shortcuts' and click on* Search.

Windows Vista

What you see first

Every Windows operation takes place on the 'Desktop'. This is a virtual workspace from which you can access all the programs and files on your PC. You can choose what to place on the Desktop, either filling it with shortcut icons to your frequently used programs and folders, or leaving it free of clutter as a colourful backdrop to your work.

SEE ALSO...
- *Using the Start menu p24*
- *Create your own shortcuts p41*
- *Personalise your Desktop p42*

THE DESKTOP WINDOW

There are four main areas on the Desktop: the Taskbar (and its elements); the Desktop (background); Desktop icons and the Sidebar.

Taskbar

Running along the bottom of the Desktop screen, the Taskbar contains the Start button and Quick Launch Toolbar (see page 11) on the left, and the 'notification area' on the far right. As you open new windows, they will appear as buttons on the Taskbar. You can reduce, or 'minimise', a window on the Desktop to a button on the Taskbar so that you can see other items. To do this, simply click on the – button (left) near the top right-hand

corner of a window. To view the window again, click on its associated button on the Taskbar and it will be restored.

Start button

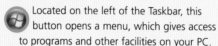 Located on the left of the Taskbar, this button opens a menu, which gives access to programs and other facilities on your PC.

Quick Launch Toolbar

This toolbar allows you to 'launch' programs with a single mouse click but it may be hidden, depending on how Windows is set up. If it is not already displayed, follow the instructions on page 11 to view it. You can also drag icons here to make shortcuts.

Notification area

This holds a variety of useful icons, depending on what software and utilities are installed. The permanent ones are Volume Control and the Clock. Any extra items not in use are hidden, but can be viewed by clicking on the arrow button, to their left.

Sidebar

A long vertical bar displayed on the right of your Desktop. It contains mini-programs called 'gadgets'. By default it displays a clock, news feed headlines and a slide show. You can add additional gadgets, such as a weather report, to the Sidebar (see panel below).

Close up
You can have the Taskbar hide itself automatically when you don't need it. Right-click on the Taskbar and choose Properties. *Put a tick next to 'Auto-hide the taskbar' and click on* OK. *To see the Taskbar again, just move your mouse pointer to the bottom of the screen and it will pop up.*

Adding gadgets
To add a new gadget to your Sidebar, move your mouse to the top of the bar and click on the '+'. To add, say, the Weather gadget, right-click on it and click on **Add** in the pop-up menu. To customise it (to change the location on the weather report, for example), right-click on the gadget and select **Options**. Type in the location you want and click on **OK**.

YOUR DESKTOP

If you have a new PC or have installed Windows Vista from scratch, you may only be able to see the Recycle Bin icon. Follow the instructions on page 10 to display the icons shown below.

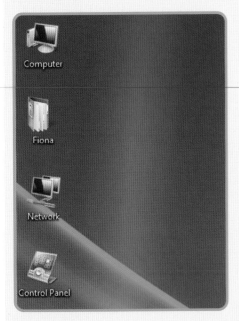

Desktop icons

These icons give you quick access to important areas on your hard disk, networked PCs and the Control Panel. You can add extra shortcuts to the Desktop for any important files and folders (see page 41), but it's a good idea not to let it get too cluttered. To access a feature

represented by an icon, place your mouse pointer on it and double-click with the left button. The standard Desktop icons associated with Vista are featured below.

Computer

You can open all the drives on your computer from this icon, including the hard drive, a CD or DVD drive. You can then access all of the files and folders inside them by double-clicking on the icons.

User's Files

Each user – here Fiona – has his or her own folder. To access it, double-click on the folder icon or click on the Start button and then on 'Fiona'. This is the default location in which Windows will suggest you save your files, in various dedicated folders.

To make it work more efficiently for you, learn how to create folders within folders (see page 33). Windows may automatically create folders for you, depending on the Windows software you use: Music is used by Media Player to store your MP3 and other music files; Pictures is for your images from a scanner or digital camera; and Downloads stores files you have downloaded from the Internet.

Network

If your computer is on a network – for example, you may have two or more PCs in your home linked by a communications cable – you can 'see' and access them through this facility. You can then share and transfer files between them, and even share a printer or modem.

Control Panel

Use the Control Panel to make changes to the Windows settings, including the colour and appearance of your Desktop and windows, hardware and software setup and configuration, and security.

Recycle Bin

Drag documents into the bin when you have no more use for them. They are stored here until you empty the bin. This allows you to make a final check before you delete them or to bring them back into use.

Bright idea
You can move icons on the Desktop anywhere you want them. By default, they should 'snap' to an invisible grid. If they don't do this, right-click on a blank area of the Desktop, select View *and put a tick next to 'Align to Grid'.*

Expert advice
Depending on whether you upgraded to or installed Windows Vista, your Desktop, its icons and the Taskbar may look slightly different from the images in this book. However, they should all work in the same way.

Moving around a window

The Explorer window that appears when you double-click on a disk or folder icon provides you with a number of options. Most importantly, it displays the contents of the disk or folder you opened and allows you to open files contained within it. It also gives access to some key functions with just one click, and presents some quick navigation routes.

SEE ALSO...
● *Using Windows Explorer* p26
● *Arranging windows* p28

A TYPICAL WINDOW
Double-clicking on a Windows folder will open a standard window which has several key elements.

The Title bar area
This is the pale coloured area at the top of a window, above the Address bar (see page 23). Depending what you are viewing, it may display the name of the program along with the name of the document – at other times, this area may remain blank. The colour of the Windows border running along the top of the Title bar

indicates whether the window is active (dark shading) or not (light shading). The shading changes are subtle, but the 'Close' button provides another indicator – if its background is red, the window is active.

You can only work within an active window – to activate an inactive window, just click on it. To move a window to see and access other items on the Desktop, click on the Title bar area at the top of the window and, keeping the left mouse button pressed, drag the window. To

 refresh the contents of a window click on the 'up and down' arrow icon to the right of the Address bar.

Sizing buttons
At the top right of a window, three icons allow

 you to minimise, maximise, restore and close the window. Click on the **Minimize** button

to hide the window. It becomes a button on the Taskbar at the bottom of the screen. To view the window again, just click once on the

 'Taskbar' button. Clicking on the **Maximize** button enlarges the window to fill the entire screen, and the border becomes black.

 After this, the button changes from a single square to two overlapping squares, becoming

 the **Restore Down** button. Click on it to return the window to its previous size. On the far right, you can click on the **Close** button to shut the window or quit the program.

If you have been working on a document or file and have not saved your work since making some changes, the computer will ask you if you want to save the file before it allows the program to close.

Bright idea
You can maximise a window or restore it to its original size quickly by double-clicking on the window's Title bar.

Watch out
When a program is minimised, a common mistake is to restart the program to see it. However, this will result in two versions of the program running at the same time. To restore a program window once it has been minimised, click once on its button on the Taskbar.

WITHIN THE WINDOW

Navigating icons and menus is easy once you know what options are available and where to find them.

Menu bar

The Menu bar displays a series of words that are headings for drop-down menus, each of which lists related commands. Click on a

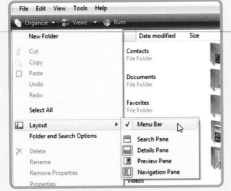

heading to view the menu. If this bar is not visible, click on the **Organize** button, go to **Layout** and then select **Menu Bar**.

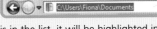

Address bar

The Address bar at the top of each folder view displays the current folder address as a set of names separated by

arrows, and offers a way to navigate between folders. To select a sub-folder in the Address bar, click on the right-pointing arrow to the right of that folder. Click on one of the sub-folders to open it instead of the current folder.

The 'Back' and 'Forward' arrow buttons to the left of the Address bar let you cycle through windows you have viewed and the downward pointing button to the right of these displays the previous folders viewed. If the current folder

is in the list, it will be highlighted in bold. Click in the empty space to the right of the names in the Address bar to reveal the full folder path. If you want to refresh the display click on the 'up and down' arrow button to the right of the Address bar.

Navigation pane

The 'Navigation' pane at the left of a folder or drive window includes links to drives, folders, favourites, and other related tasks depending on what is selected within the window. Click on a folder in the 'Navigation' pane on the left to reveal its contents in the pane on the right.

Details Pane

The 'Details Pane' at the bottom of a window displays information about the selected item in the panes above.

Borders and scroll bars

These frame the window, enabling you to resize or scroll around within it. When you place the cursor on the border of a window, it changes to a two-headed arrow. At this point, click and drag to resize the window. Doing this at a corner allows you to resize the width and the height of the window together. Move around the screen to the left and right or up and down by clicking on the appropriate arrows on the scroll bars. Alternatively, click and drag the light blue scroll box in the desired direction.

Change the display

Click on the **Views** button on the toolbar to change how the contents of a folder is displayed. Each time you click on the button, the contents of the selected folder is viewed using the next view in the sequence: by Icon, List, Details and Tiles. Click on the downward pointing arrow to the right of the 'Views' button for extra viewing options ('Extra Large', 'Large', 'Medium' and 'Small' icons).

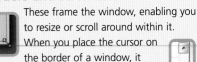

Close up
If you are not sure what a button on a toolbar represents, try letting your mouse pointer hover over it for a second. A small 'ToolTip' message will then appear showing the button's name, providing a useful hint.

Close up
The Views button allows you to choose how to display the contents of a folder: Icon displays the files as icons with no file information; List displays the files as tiny icons in list form; Details lists information such as a file's size and creation date; and Tiles displays files as large icons with the file type and size.

Using the Start menu

The Start button is a fast way to access the key programs, documents and files on your PC. By default, it is located in the bottom left-hand corner of the screen. Click on it once to open the Start menu, and then select an item, such as 'Internet Explorer', to launch it. The All Programs arrow displays further submenus, containing entries for all the programs on your PC.

SEE ALSO...
● *Personalise your Desktop* *p42*

START MENU BASICS

From the Start button you are only ever a couple of clicks away from all the programs and files on your computer.

 Click on the large black arrow to the left of 'All Programs' to open a submenu. Here you'll see a list of the programs on your PC. Often you'll see a smaller arrow next to an item, such as 'Accessories'. Click on the item to see its submenu. Above 'All Programs' is a quick-access list of your most recently used programs as well as icons for the Internet and e-mail.

 Select **Recent Items** to view a submenu of the last 15 files you worked on. Click on one to open the document in the program that created it.

 Click on **Control Panel** to adjust your computer's settings, such as 'Date and Time', 'Sounds' and 'Display'.

 **Default Programs** changes the default program Windows uses to open certain files such as pictures.

 **Help and Support** has a searchable index of advice. You will require Internet access for some information.

 Select **Search** to find files on your PC. See page 36 to learn how to use the search function.

The circled button sends your PC into 'Power Save'; the 'Lock' button secures your PC, requiring a password to 'unlock' it. The arrow gives additional 'Turn Off' options (see opposite).

Close up
If you can't see the 'Recent Items' icon on your Start menu, right-click on the Taskbar and choose Properties. *Then click on the* Start Menu *tab and put a tick next to 'Store and display a list of recently opened files'.*

A CLOSER LOOK

Familiarise yourself with the 'Turn Off' option, customise your Start menu and learn how to use 'paths'.

Shutting down your PC options

Click on the **Start** button and select the button on the far right at the bottom of the black panel. There are six options to choose from:

Switch User – use this to select a different user from the Welcome screen, without logging off.

Log Off – use this when you have finished using the PC but don't want to shut it down.

Lock is the same as clicking on the 'padlock' button. The Welcome screen will appear and a password must be entered for you to return to your account.

Restart closes down your computer and then restarts it. This is useful after new programs have been installed, or if you are experiencing glitches.

Sleep puts your PC to 'sleep' to save power. Move the mouse or press a key to 'wake' it up.

Shut Down closes all programs, saves Windows' settings and turns off the PC.

Customise the Start menu

To alter the Start menu so that it meets your needs, right-click on a blank section of the Taskbar and select **Properties** from the pop-up menu. Click on the **Start Menu** tab and then click on the **Customize** button.

Scroll through the items to customise in the main panel, checking and unchecking them as you go. Select from the options under each

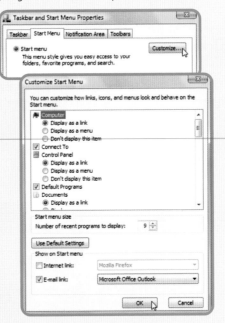

heading for how you want to display that item. Below, choose the number of program icons that will be visible and whether you wish to have Internet and e-mail links shown at the top of the Start menu.

If, for instance, you want to add a submenu to the Control Panel, click on 'Display as a menu'. When you're finished, click on **OK** to close the Customize Start Menu dialogue box and then on **OK** again to close the Properties dialogue box.

How do I change the way the Start menu looks?

If you want to know more about customising the Start Menu, click on the link at the bottom of the Taskbar and Start Menu Properties dialogue box. You will then be presented with the 'Help and Support' page 'Customize the Start menu'. Click on the blue links for more information.

Use the Run feature

By selecting **Run**, you can launch anything you have on your PC, including programs, CDs and DVDs. To use it, open Taskbar and Start Menu Properties as before, scroll through the list and click on **Run command**, then on **OK**.

If you already know where the item you want to launch is stored on your computer, you can type in the route to the file, known as the 'path', and then click on **OK**. For instance, the path to the program WinZip might be 'C:\Users\ Fiona/Downloads\winzip111.exe'. 'C:' is the drive that WinZip is on, while 'Downloads' is the folder in which it is stored. If you don't know the path to the file you want to open, click on the **Browse** button to search your computer for it.

Bright idea
If you want to add a frequently used program to the top section of the Start menu, drag it from its program menu to the Start *button and then up to the required position.*

Using Windows Explorer

Unlike some earlier versions of Windows, the tools and features of Windows Explorer appear every time you open a folder or double-click on a disk drive in Windows Vista. This facility allows you to access your file and folder system easily and efficiently, and also helps you to organise and sort the files in a way that suits your needs.

SEE ALSO...
- *File your work p32*
- *Finding files p38*

To access the Windows Explorer tools, click on the Start menu and choose Documents. Then click on the 'Organize' button on the Toolbar.

What you see

A typical Explorer window is divided into two panes. On the left-hand side is a list of the drives and folders on your PC. When you click on one of these, the files and folders it contains

are displayed in the right-hand pane. This means that you can search through the entire contents of your computer in a single window.

The left-hand pane is for navigating around your computer. Click on the open triangle to the left of a drive or a folder to expand the contents of that drive or folder. Click on the black triangle to collapse the contents again. This makes it much easier to scroll through the list when you're looking for your files. If there is no triangle, that folder contains only files, which are

displayed in the right-hand pane. Click on a folder or file in the right-hand pane and a summarised description of that selected item will appear in the bottom of the window. The summary will tell you what the item is, when it was last modified, its size and, if it is a file, the name of the author. If you do not see this detail, click on the **Organize** button, scroll down to **Layout** and click on **Details Pane**.

Bright idea
If you regularly work on the same file, right-click on it in any folder window and select Send To*, then* Desktop (create shortcut)*. This places a shortcut icon on the Desktop which, when double-clicked, will open your file.*

LOOKING CLOSER

When you are familiar with Windows Explorer, it is easy to navigate your hard disk and reorganise your files.

Sorting files and folders

There are four main ways to view the data on the right-hand side of the Explorer window: by Icon (Extra Large, Large, Medium and Small), List, Details and Tiles. To select an option, click on the **View** menu or click on the **Views** button on the toolbar (see page 23 for information). Select **Details** for the most comprehensive viewing option – you'll see the file name, size and type, and the date and time

it was last saved. No matter how you choose to view your files and folders, you can alter the order in which they are displayed. Click on the **View** menu and then **Sort by**. The submenu gives you several options:

Name displays files in alphabetical order, with the folders grouped together at the top or

bottom of the list. In all cases, the order can be changed by clicking on the small arrow to the right of the column name.

Size arranges folders by name in ascending alphabetical order, and then files by size, with the smallest file first.

Type groups files of the same kind – such as graphics files or Word documents – in ascending alphabetical order. Folders are placed at the bottom of the list.

Date modified sorts folders and files with the most recently modified files at the top.

Two further options are **Group By** which organises your files in like groups according to the submenu option you choose; and **Stack By**. If you then choose **Name** from the submenu, they are categorised into alphabetical groups, A–H, I–P and Q–Z.

Changing views

If you choose the Details view and have not selected the 'Show in Groups' option, you'll see that the sort order is indicated by a small arrow beside the column heading. You can sort your files by a different category by clicking on a

column heading in the Name bar. Clicking on the heading again reverses the sort order.

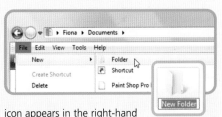

Organising your work

Folders are a good way to group your files together. To create a new folder, choose where you want it to go by clicking once on the appropriate folder or drive icon in the left-hand pane of Explorer. Now click on the **File** menu and select **New**, then **Folder**. A new folder

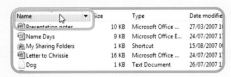

icon appears in the right-hand pane with the name 'New Folder' highlighted. Type a folder name and press **Return**. You can now drag and drop files into this folder. In the right pane, locate the file you want to put in the new folder. Then find your folder in the left pane, by opening other folders until you can see it. Don't click on the folder you want. Click on the file on the right and drag it onto your folder's icon on the left. When the folder is highlighted, release the mouse button to complete the action.

Customising folders

You can change the appearance of folders in Windows Explorer to help identify files belonging to different users. Open the folder you want to change. Click on the **View** menu and select **Customize This Folder**. You can choose a picture to go on your folder, or change the icon to make it more recognisable. The picture will not be visible in the List or Details views though.

Arranging windows

The Windows Desktop can easily become filled with open program and folder windows – for example, a letter in progress, your e-mail Inbox, or a spreadsheet of monthly expenses. However, with a little organisation, you can resize and switch between windows quickly and easily, and still stay focused on the task in hand.

SEE ALSO...
- *Using the Start menu p24*
- *Using Windows Explorer p26*
- *Create your own shortcuts p41*

BEFORE YOU START
Open up a few windows on your Desktop, such as a letter, an e-mail *program, and your Documents folder. You can then experiment as you go through the steps.*

1 If you need to move an open window on your screen – so you can see it while working in another window, for instance – click on the **Title bar** at the top of the window and drag it across to wherever you would like it. If your windows are the wrong size, you can resize them by clicking on any of the corners or sides; the mouse pointer turns into a double-headed arrow and you can then drag windows inwards or outwards to the new size.

2 The easiest way to work with multiple windows is to have only one of them visible at a time. If there are any windows you are not using, click on their **Minimize** buttons (in the upper right-hand corner).

Each minimised window is shown as a button on the Taskbar. If six or more files are open in the same program, their Taskbar buttons will be reduced to one button with the number of windows on it. Click on it and a list pops up.

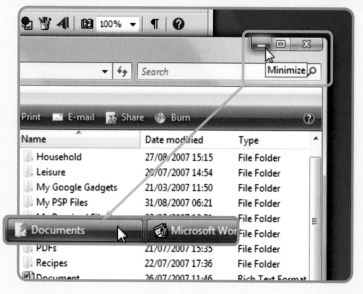

Customise your Taskbar

You can move your Taskbar to the sides or top of your screen. Click on the **Taskbar** near, but not on, the Start button, and drag it to where you want. To make the Taskbar bigger, position the mouse on the line between

the top of the Taskbar and the Desktop (left). When it changes into a double-headed arrow, click and drag the **Taskbar** upwards. Note, you need to unlock the Taskbar first, see page 11.

That's amazing!
Right-click on the **Taskbar** and select **Toolbars** to choose from a range of options. You can convert your Desktop icons to buttons on the Taskbar, show an Address bar for Web addresses, or even display a list of Internet links.

---

4 If you have three or more windows open, right-click on the **Taskbar** and select **Cascade Windows**. This makes the windows overlap slightly so you can view all the Title bars at once (below). Or, to clear the Desktop of all windows, click on the **Show the Desktop** button and all the windows will instantly be reduced to buttons on your Taskbar.

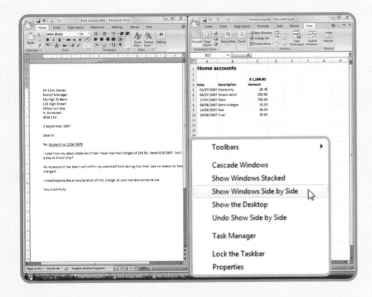

3 If you're working with two related documents in different programs, it can help to have the two windows side by side on screen. To do this, open both documents, right-click on the **Taskbar** and choose **Show** **Windows Side by Side**. You can now work in either window simply by clicking anywhere in it. Note that if you choose 'Show Windows Stacked', the windows will occupy the top and bottom halves of the Desktop.

Expert advice
To switch off the live windows previews in Windows Aero, right-click on the Taskbar and select **Properties**. Then click on the box marked 'Show window previews (thumbnails)' to uncheck it.

6 Windows Aero groups together windows from the same program on a single button on the Taskbar. Click on this button to view a list of the window titles and hover the mouse pointer over an entry to see a thumbnail image. If you prefer not to have buttons grouped, right-click on the Taskbar and select **Properties**, then click on **Group similar taskbar buttons** to uncheck the box.

5 Windows Vista has a useful new feature called Windows Aero to help organise your work. When a window has been minimised to a button on the Taskbar, you can view a thumbnail preview of it by hovering your mouse pointer over the button.

Bright idea
Press Ctrl + Windows key + Tab to keep Flip 3D open. You can then press Tab (without holding down any other key) to cycle through the windows.

Close up
In Flip 3D, one of the icons or previews displayed will be for the Desktop itself, giving you a quick way to show the Desktop and minimise the other Windows.

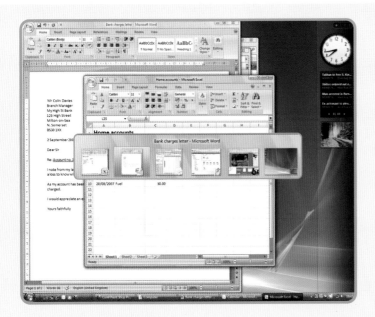

8 Windows Flip 3D offers another visually dramatic way to switch between windows. Press and hold down the **Windows key** and then press **Tab**. Your open windows are now displayed in a 3D stack. Press the **Tab** key repeatedly, or rotate the mouse wheel to cycle through the windows. Release the Windows key to display the window at the front of the stack.

7 Windows Vista allows you to switch between open windows using its new 'Windows Flip' feature. Press and hold down the **Alt** key, then press the **Tab** key. Your open windows are now displayed in a bar running from left to right across the middle of the screen. With the **Alt** key held down, press the **Tab** key until the window you want is highlighted, and then release it.

File your work

Your hard disk is like a virtual filing cabinet: each document is stored in a folder, as are all the programs you use. Also, folders can be stored in other folders, like drawers in a cabinet. It's tempting to keep all your documents on your Windows Desktop where you can see them but, as with a real desk, life is much easier if you avoid clutter and confusion.

SEE ALSO...
● *What is Windows?* *p10*
● *Using Windows Explorer* *p26*
● *Deleting files* *p36*
● *Maintain your hard disk* *p46*

CREATING FOLDERS
There are several ways to create new folders. The method you use depends on how and where you save your work. Here are three ways to make a new folder.

1 Always create new folders for your work within the Documents folder, or in a folder inside Documents. First, click on the **Start** button and choose **Documents**. Then click on the **File** menu and select **New** then **Folder**. It's also possible to add a new folder inside an existing folder. To do this, find the folder within Documents and double-click on it before creating your new one.

2 Your new folder will appear in the right-hand pane. The highlighted name, 'New Folder', is the default name and will be replaced as soon as you begin typing in your preferred folder name. Choose a recognisable and memorable name for your new folder and then press the **Return** key.

Finding lost files

If you can't find a file or folder, click on the **Start** button, then on **Search**. Type the file name, or as much of it as you can remember, in the 'Search' box at the top right. As you start typing, matching files and folders are displayed in the right pane below. Hover your mouse pointer over a match for more detail.

Expert advice

Always name your files logically so that, if you forget a file's full name, you can still perform a search for it. If several family members use your PC, you can still create folders for each person. Use names or initials when naming documents to distinguish one person's files from another.

3 You can also create a new folder within the Documents folder while you are saving. Open a document, click on **File** and choose **Save As**. In the Save As dialogue box click on the **New Folder** button. In the New Folder dialogue box give the folder a name, then click on **OK**. Double-click on your new folder and then click on the **Save** button to store your document inside the folder.

4 Alternatively, you can create new folders in any folder window by using your right mouse button. Open the folder in which you want to create your new folder. Then right-click on a blank area, select **New** and choose **Folder**. The default name on the folder that appears will be replaced as you type in the new name.

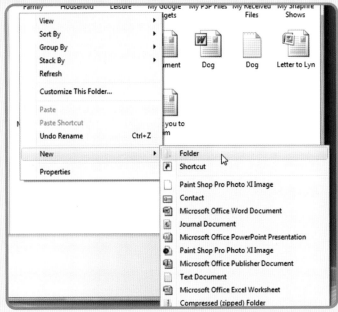

Copy and move files

There are many reasons why you may need to copy or move a file or folder – you may want to make a backup of an important document, or perhaps you need to copy files to a CD or DVD so you can transfer them to another PC. Maybe you just want to move a file to another folder on your hard disk. Whatever you want to do, Windows makes it easy.

SEE ALSO...

● *Using Windows Explorer p26*
● *File your work p32*

BEFORE YOU START
*To copy to a CD or DVD, follow the first three steps. To copy to your hard disk, open **Documents**, then click on the **Folders** button and follow the steps on page 35.*

COPYING TO A CD OR DVD

1 Insert a disc into the drive and select **Burn files to disc** in the AutoPlay window. Give your disc a title, then click on **Show formatting options**. If you want to rewrite to the disc later, choose **Live File System**. To prevent the disk being overwritten, select **Mastered** instead. Then click on **Next**.

2 Click on the **Start** button and then on **Documents**. In the left pane, navigate to the folder or file you wish to copy. In the right pane, click on the file or folder to be copied. Keep your finger pressed on the mouse button and drag the file onto the **CD/DVD** drive icon in the left pane. When the icon is highlighted, release the mouse button.

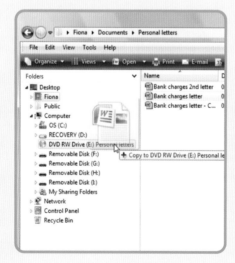

3 A dialogue box opens to show the copying progress. If you see that you are copying the wrong file, or the right file to the wrong place, click on **Cancel**. When finished, click on **Close session** from the **File** menu and remove the disc from the drive.

Moving files

As with a conventional paper filing system, you will often want to move your files and folders. Windows helps you do this. Click on the file or folder and, keeping your finger pressed down on the left mouse button, drag it over to the new location. When the destination folder is highlighted, release the mouse button and the file or folder will move.

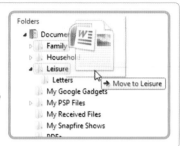

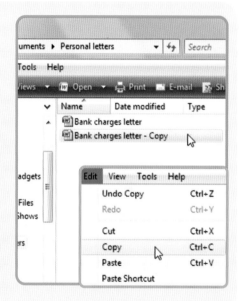

Watch out

When you drag a file from one drive to another – from your hard disk to the CD or DVD drive, for example – you are left with two identical files: one on the original drive and an exact copy on the destination drive. If you drag a file to a different place on the same drive, the file will just move, without making a copy.

MAKING COPIES OF FILES

1 To make a copy of a file that is stored on your hard disk, first open the folder that contains the file that you wish to copy. Then click on the file once to select it, click on the **Edit** menu and select **Copy**.

2 Now locate the folder into which you wish to paste a copy of the selected file. Double-click on it, then click on the **Edit** menu and select **Paste**. An exact copy of the file will appear in the right-hand pane of the window.

3 You can also store a copy of a file within the same folder as the original. Click on the relevant file, click on the **Edit** menu, select **Copy** and then click on **Edit** again followed by **Paste**. To distinguish the copy, Windows appends ' - Copy' to the name of your original file.

Deleting files

Regardless of how fast or powerful your computer is, it will begin to slow down if the hard disk gets too full. There will also be less disk space available for new files and programs. It's therefore a good idea to delete redundant files and folders regularly, moving them from your hard disk to the Recycle Bin. This, in turn, needs to be emptied to free up the disk space.

SEE ALSO...
- *Maximise your disk space p44*
- *Maintain your hard disk p46*

THROWING ITEMS AWAY

It's easy to dump unwanted files or folders in the Recycle Bin. And if you throw one away by mistake, you can retrieve it just as quickly.

Delete options

There are a number of ways to put an item in the Recycle Bin: you can drag and drop the file or folder onto the 'Recycle Bin' icon; select the file and

press the **Delete** key on the keyboard; or right-click on the file and choose **Delete**. When you choose to delete a file (unless you drag it to the bin), Windows will ask you if you are sure you want to do this. Click on the **Yes** button to confirm the action. Note, the 'Recycle Bin' icon will be hidden if you are in a maximised window, so you will not be able to use the drag and drop method to delete an item.

The Desktop icon shows an empty bin when there is nothing in it and displays contents in the bin when it contains files. You can view the contents of the Recycle Bin by double-clicking on it. Putting files in the bin does not free up disk space, as the files are still stored on your hard drive. In order to free up the space, you must empty the

Recycle Bin. With the Recycle Bin window open, you can see a list of its contents in the right-hand pane, with options for emptying the bin and restoring files on the dark-coloured menu bar above. Click on **Empty the Recycle Bin** to permanently delete all the files. If you do not want to delete all the files in one go, select the ones you know that you no longer want, click on the **File** menu and choose **Delete**. You will need to confirm your action.

Restoring files

Open the Recycle Bin and select **Restore all items** from the dark-coloured Menu bar. This will return the files to their original locations on your PC. If you just want to restore one file, select it and click on **Restore this item**.

Bright idea
If you want to delete a few files at the same time, select them all by clicking on the first file, holding down the Ctrl key and the clicking on the others in turn. You can then delete them collectively using the methods described above.

Watch out
Files deleted from a CD, DVD or other removable storage media will not be placed in the Recycle Bin. Also files too large for the Bin will be deleted immediately. If this is the case, Windows will display a warning box.

THE RECYCLE BIN PROPERTIES

The storage capacity of the Recycle Bin can be increased or decreased to suit your requirements – but you may need to take the size of your hard drive into consideration.

Adjusting the capacity of the bin

Right-click on the **Recycle Bin** icon, choose **Properties** and, with the **General** tab selected, you can determine just what proportion of the hard disk you are prepared to allocate to the storage of files in the Recycle Bin.

The 'Custom size' box gives the default size of your hard disk. You can increase the hard disk space by typing a higher figure into the box. If you work with lots of large files, you may want to increase the figure to 25% of its original size to allow for their storage. But you should bear in mind that if you allocate a lot of hard disk space to the Recycle Bin, you must empty it regularly or it will gradually fill up your hard disk. This may result in your PC slowing down

and eventually you will receive a warning that disk space is low. When you reach the limit of your Recycle Bin's storage capacity, your PC will automatically begin to delete the files in the bin, starting with the oldest ones.

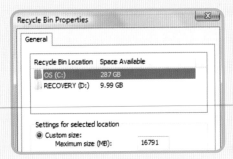

Deliberate deletion

If you wish, you can get rid of the Confirm File Delete dialogue box that appears when you move a file or folder to the bin. In the Recycle Bin Properties dialogue box, remove the tick next to 'Display delete confirmation dialog', then click

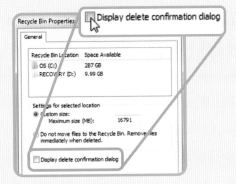

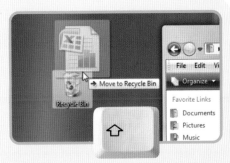

on **Apply** and **OK**. Your files or folders will now go straight into the Recycle Bin.

If you are sure that you will never need a file again, hold down the **Shift** key when you drag it into the Recycle Bin (above). The Confirm File Delete dialogue box does not appear and the file is deleted without being held in the bin.

Alternatively, you can put a tick next to 'Do not move files to the Recycle Bin. Remove files immediately when deleted' in the 'Recycle Bin Properties' box. Only use these methods if you are confident that you no longer need your documents because, once you have done this, the files can only be recovered with the help of specialist software, such as Norton Utilities.

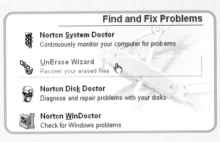

That's amazing!

Even the most basic computers now come with 80–160GB hard disks – on more expensive models they can be as much as 320GB or 500GB. Even these huge capacities can be filled with large amounts of photos or music files, however. It is therefore good practice to delete old files on a regular basis.

Finding files

Once you have been using your computer for a while you may build up a large collection of files and programs. Even with an efficient filing system, it is possible you may not be able to find a document that you need. Windows Vista's Search facility not only allows you to locate files on your PC, but also enables you to find Web sites and information via the Internet.

SEE ALSO...
- *Using Windows Explorer p26*
- *File your work p32*

THE SEARCH IS ON

Regardless of how many files are stored on your PC, Windows can locate any one of them quickly – even if you're not sure of the file name.

Locating files

If you are having trouble finding a specific file, the first place to look for it is in your Documents folder. If you can remember in which folder you normally save your work – for instance, 'Letters' or 'Personal Files' – then that's the first place to look.

If your file isn't there, and you know that it was worked on recently, click on the **Start** button and then on **Recent Items**. This lists the last 15 files that were opened on your computer, even if you did not make any changes to them. If the file you want is listed, click on it once to open it. If neither of these

methods proves successful, you may have accidentally saved your file in the wrong folder or dragged it to the Recycle Bin. In this case you will need to use the Windows Search tool.

Searching in the Start menu

The Start menu gives you a very easy way to locate files, folders and programs. Click on the **Start** button, then start typing a word that you

know is part of the document you want, for example, 'letter'. There is no need to click in the box. As you type, relevant files, folders and programs appear in the left-hand pane, replacing the normal display of programs. When the one you want appears, click on it to open the file in its associated program.

Close up
If you click on the Search button on any folder toolbar, it opens the Search For Files and Folders facility in the left-hand pane of the folder window.

That's amazing!
If you have forgotten a file's full name, you can use the '*' symbol (type **Shift + 8**) to search for it. When you use the asterisk in a search, it represents any character or characters in the file name. If you only know that your file name started with an 'S', type 's*', or if your file is a Word file that ends with the name 'john', type '*john.doc'.

WINDOWS' SEARCHES

Some files are easier to find than others, so try a basic search first. If that doesn't work, use the advanced search.

Basic search

All Vista windows contain a 'Search' box in the top right corner, so finding files and folders is very easy. Type your search word or words into the search bar. As you type, matches from the current folder and its sub-folders will begin to appear in the right-hand pane below. To select a file and open it, just double-click on the filename.

Type-specific search

If the basic search has not found your file, or has returned too many results to look through, try targeting your search more specifically. Click on the **Start** button and then on **Search**.

You will be presented with a new search window. In the 'Search' box at the top right, start typing as before. The search engine will now look at filenames and folders, and will

search inside files within your user area. To break the search down further, click on one of the options in the 'Show only' bar – limiting the search to documents or pictures, for example.

Advanced search

If you still cannot find your file, Vista provides an Advanced Search. After each search for files and folders, a prompt appears at the bottom of the right pane in the results window asking 'Did you find what you were searching for?'. Below this is an **Advanced Search** button. Click on this and an extra panel of options appears at the top of the window above the menu bar.

Did you find what you were searching for?
Advanced Search

Using this panel you can specify additional search criteria to narrow your search. Use the drop-down menus to search by 'Location', 'Date' and 'Size', or specify a name, tag or author of a file in the appropriate box. Fill in what you know and then click on **Search**. Your results will appear in the right-hand pane below.

Here is a short explanation of the 'Advanced Search' features:

Date – this is useful if you know roughly when the file was last saved.

Size – searches on the basis of file size, so if you are looking for a large image you can search for all files over, say, 1MB.

Name – enter the name of the file or folder you wish to find.

Tags – these are keywords you may have chosen to add when saving the file – they are very useful if you do need to search for it later.

Authors – this is the name of the originator of the document and anyone else who has modified it.

Sorting your results

When a search is complete, your results will be listed in the order in which Search located them. This is because Search looks in a specific sequence of locations. Click on the **Type** column heading above the file names to see the results grouped together by type, with folders first, followed by any relevant files. Click on the **Type** heading again to view the results in reverse alphabetical order.

Watch out
Remember that, with all searches, if you type in 'count' search will also find 'account', 'accountant' and 'accountancy'.

Quick keyboard commands

Nearly all the actions or commands you perform with your mouse can also be done by pressing 'hot keys' – these are single keys or combinations of keys. For example, you can access the Start menu by pressing the 'Windows' key at the bottom left of your keyboard, or you can open 'Computer' by pressing the 'Windows' and 'E' keys together.

HANDY HOT KEYS

Use key commands to select menu options and navigate Windows.

Selecting main menu options

The menu bars in Windows programs all look similar and contain common menus such as 'File', 'Edit' and 'View'. On these menu bars, one letter is underlined in each menu item, for example, 'File' or 'Format'. In Windows Explorer you have to press the **Alt** key (to the left of the Spacebar on the keyboard) to see these letters.

In any window, press **Alt** followed by the underlined letter in the menu item to open the menu:

Alt + **F** to open the File menu
Alt + **E** to open the Edit menu
Alt + **V** to open the View menu
Alt + **A** to open the Favorites menu
Alt + **T** to open the Tools menu
Alt + **H** to open the Help menu.

Using the Function keys

The Function keys, also known as the 'F keys', at the top of the keyboard perform preset actions. For example, press **F1** to access a program's Help database. From the Windows Desktop, press **F3** to access the Search Results dialogue box. You can also use Function keys in combination with other keys. To close a window or program, for example, press the **Alt** and **F4** keys together.

Moving around the Desktop

You can use keyboard shortcuts to move around your Desktop. For example, click anywhere on the Desktop, then press the arrow keys to move to any icon (they are highlighted when selected). Press the **Return** key to open the selected item.

The same principle can be applied inside folders. Open the Documents folder then press the arrow keys to move around the folder's contents. Press **Return** when you want to open a selected file or folder.

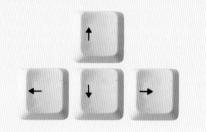

Important command keys

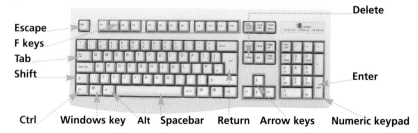

Escape
F keys
Tab
Shift

Delete

Enter

Ctrl   Windows key   Alt   Spacebar   Return   Arrow keys   Numeric keypad

Close up
If several programs are open, use the Alt and Tab keys to select one. Hold down Alt *and then press* Tab *and a bar shows the program icons – the active one is outlined. Move through the icons by pressing* Tab, *and release* Alt *to make the outlined program active. See page 31 for more details.*

Create your own shortcuts

O nce you have an understanding of Windows and its programs, you can create 'shortcuts' to help you work more quickly. A shortcut is an icon on your Desktop or Taskbar, or an entry on your Start menu, that is linked to a program, file or folder. The shortcut launches the related item immediately, which saves you searching through multiple menus or folders.

QUICK LINKS

Create shortcuts to folders, documents and programs for quick and easy access.

Extra programs in the Start menu

You can add a program to the top of the Start menu simply by dragging the program icon onto it from its location under 'All Programs'. Locate the item to which you want to add a shortcut, click on it and hold down the left button while you drag it to a new position above the grey line in the Start menu. Let go and the shortcut will appear.

Program shortcuts on your Desktop

To make a shortcut to a program, right-click anywhere on the **Desktop**, select **New** and click on **Shortcut**. In the Create Shortcut window that appears, click on the **Browse** button.

Locate the relevant program in the Browse for Files or Folders dialogue box by clicking on the folders and drives under 'Select the target of the shortcut below'. Scroll down and click on relevant folders to open them. Select the program, click on **OK** and click on the **Next** button. Choose a name and click on the **Finish** button. The shortcut, which looks like the program icon with a small arrow, appears on your Desktop.

Desktop documents

You can also create Desktop shortcuts for documents that you use regularly. Locate the file in its folder and right-click on it. Click on **Send To** on the pop-up menu and then choose **Desktop (create shortcut)**. A shortcut icon appears on the Desktop. Drag and drop the shortcut wherever you like on the Desktop.

An alternative method is to drag the item to your **Desktop** while holding down the right mouse button instead of the left button. When you let go, a pop-up menu appears. Choose **Create Shortcuts Here** to put the shortcut on your Desktop. Now, to open the document, just double-click on the shortcut icon.

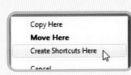

The ultimate time-saver

Set up a program to launch when you start your PC. Click on the **Start** button and choose **Computer**. In the right-hand pane, find the program on the hard disk. Drag the program over your **Start** button without letting go. Hover the mouse there and the Start menu will open. Now hover the icon over **All Programs** and, when its submenu opens, drag the icon to **Startup** and then to its submenu. Now release the mouse button. This 'drops' the program and puts a shortcut into the Startup folder.

Close up

To remove a program shortcut, click on it and drag it onto the Recycle Bin. This won't delete the program itself, which is still in the Program Files folder, because the shortcut is just a link to it.

Personalise your Desktop

The Windows Desktop is part of your working environment and so it is important you like its appearance and colour scheme. Fortunately, you can change the background image on the Windows Desktop and the colour of the window frames with just a few clicks. You can also choose from a range of animated screensavers for when you're not using your PC.

SEE ALSO...
● *Create your own shortcuts p41*

DESKTOP MAKEOVER

Windows comes with an extensive selection of Desktop backgrounds.

Background images

To change your Desktop background, right-click anywhere on your Desktop and select **Personalize** from the pop-up menu. In the window that appears, click on the **Desktop Background** link. With 'Windows Wallpapers' selected in the 'Picture Location' options, scroll through the list of available images. Click on one that interests you and your Desktop will automatically change to that image. If the image doesn't fill your screen or you would prefer it to display differently, click on one of the options beneath the pictures. Select **Stretch** (on the left) to force the image to fit the screen,

Tile (in the middle) to repeat the image over your Desktop or **Center** (on the right) to position the image in the centre of the Desktop. When you have made your choice, click on **OK**.

USING YOUR OWN PICTURES

You can use your own digital photographs, stored on the hard disk, as your Desktop background.

A truly personal Desktop

Make sure you store any pictures you have downloaded, scanned or taken using a digital camera in your Pictures folder – you can find this inside your Documents folder. Your pictures will then be available for easy selection from the 'Pictures' option, as they will appear in the 'Picture Location' drop-down list.

If you want to use pictures which are stored in another folder, click on the **Browse** button. Locate the folder containing your photograph, click on it to select it, and then click on **Open**. The image will now be displayed. Select a positioning option as previously described and click on **OK** to confirm your choice.

Bright idea

Remind yourself of an important message using a screen saver. In the Personalization window, click on the Screen Saver link, choose the 3D Text screen saver and click on the Settings button. Then type your reminder, and select a font, colour and style. Choose how fast it scrolls across your screen, then click on OK and OK again.

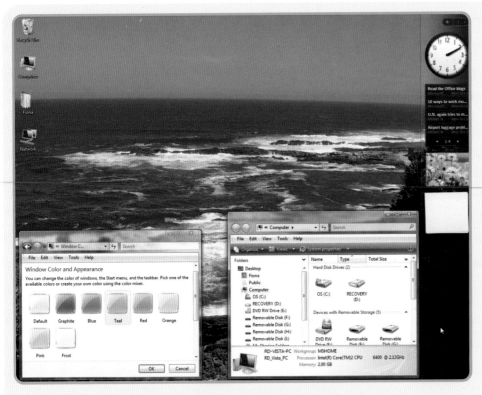

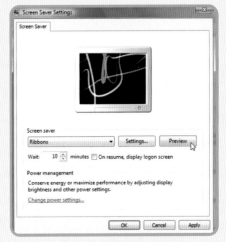

MOVING PICTURES

Screen savers are animations that appear when your PC is idle. They can also protect work from prying eyes.

Small-screen animation

To select a screen saver, right-click anywhere on the **Desktop** and select **Personalize** from the pop-up menu. Click on the **Screen Saver** link and then click on the down arrow to the right of the box under 'Screen saver'. Scroll through the list and select an option. Click on **Preview**

COLOUR SCHEMES

Windows lets you choose different colour schemes for your Desktop.

More than just a Desktop

Open the Personalization window and click on the **Window Color and Appearance** link. Here you can choose from eight preset Windows colours, including the default.

Click on the 'Enable transparency' option to give your windows a 'glass-like' appearance. You can also click and drag on the 'Color intensity' slider to vary the depth of colour.

to view your choice on screen. To return to the Screen Saver Settings dialogue box, just move your mouse a little. You can now set the length of time your PC waits before activating the screen saver in the 'Wait' box. Finally, click on **OK** to confirm your choices.

Save your energy

On some PCs, the Screen Saver Settings dialogue box has a power management option that reduces the amount of power used by your monitor and/or hard disk after a set period of inactivity. Click on the **Change power settings** link and the Power Options dialogue box opens. Here you can select a power plan or change its settings. To make a change, click on the **Change plan settings** link, and select the time to 'Turn off the display' and 'Put the computer to sleep' from the drop-down lists.

Maximise your disk space

As you create more and more files and install new programs on your PC, your hard disk will start to fill up. If your hard disk gets too full, you will run out of room to install further programs and your PC may slow down. Keep an eye on how much space you have and regularly delete old folders and files to help keep your PC running smoothly.

SEE ALSO...
- *Deleting files p36*
- *Maintain your hard disk p46*

BEFORE YOU START Look through your documents and decide which ones you need to keep and which ones to delete, if necessary. Make sure anything important is filed in a safe place.

1 To check how much space you have on your hard disk, click on the **Start** button and then select **Computer**. Under 'Hard Disk Drives' click on your hard drive icon, here **OS (C:)** and look in the bottom panel to make a quick check of how much free hard disk space you have.

2 Next, right-click on the **OS (C:)** icon and choose **Properties**. Under the General tab in the Properties dialogue box, you can see the amount of used and free space in more detail, as well as your hard disk capacity. This information is given in both numerical and graphical formats. Click on **OK** to close the window.

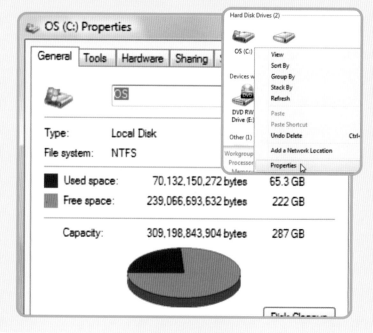

44

Bright idea
Remember to empty your Recycle Bin on a regular basis. It's amazing how quickly it can get filled with unwanted files and folders. This action can immediately free up a lot of disk space.

Close up
Windows Compressed Folders can reduce the size of certain files without losing any data. This process is known as compression. In any folder, right-click on an empty area, select New and then Compressed (zipped) Folder. Choose a suitable name and drag files to the folder to create compressed copies, and then delete the originals.

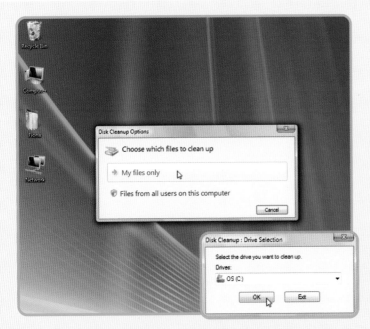

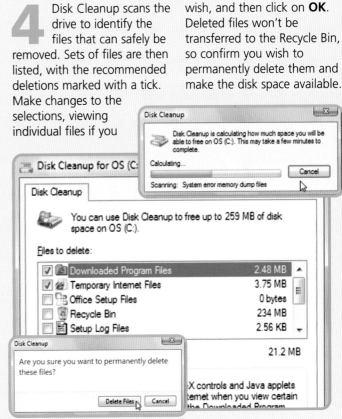

Disk Cleanup scans the drive to identify the files that can safely be removed. Sets of files are then listed, with the recommended deletions marked with a tick. Make changes to the selections, viewing individual files if you wish, and then click on **OK**. Deleted files won't be transferred to the Recycle Bin, so confirm you wish to permanently delete them and make the disk space available.

3 If you need to free up some space on your hard disk you have several options. The easiest option is to run 'Disk Cleanup'. Click on **Start**, **All Programs**, **Accessories**, **System Tools**, then **Disk Cleanup**. A prompt will ask if you want to clean your files only or all users' files. Make a choice, then select the drive to clean and click on **OK**.

Maintain your hard disk

To ensure that your hard disk is in optimum health, it's a good idea to perform regular maintenance. Windows has an error-checking program, which scans your hard disk and other drives for errors, and Disk Defragmenter, which reorders your data on the hard disk so that files are stored more efficiently. Both these utilities can help keep your PC running smoothly.

SEE ALSO...
- *Back up your work p48*
- *Computer viruses p50*

BEFORE YOU START
It can take several hours to run Disk Defragmenter, so make sure you leave plenty of time. You can leave it to run overnight, but ensure all programs are closed.

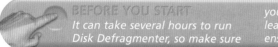

1 To check a disk for errors, click on the **Start** button and then select **Computer**. Right-click on the drive you want to check – your hard disk should be C: – and choose **Properties** from the pop-up menu. Click on the **Tools** tab and then click on the **Check Now** button under 'Error-checking'. In the Checking Disk dialogue box uncheck both 'Check disk options'. You can now perform a simple disk check by clicking on the **Start** button.

2 To perform a thorough check, put ticks next to 'Automatically fix file system errors' and 'Scan for and attempt recovery of bad sectors' in the Checking Disk dialogue box and click on **Start**.
Windows cannot check a disk drive that it is currently using, so it schedules the error-checking process to take place next time you start your computer. Click on the **Schedule disk check** button to tell Windows to go ahead.

Now close all programs and restart your computer. Before Windows has finished loading, a screen is displayed giving you the option to bypass the error check by pressing any key. If you want to go ahead with the check, simply leave your PC and the error-check will start. This process may take several minutes. The progress will be displayed on screen and your computer will restart automatically when the check is complete.

Key word
Windows often divides files into segments and stores them in various free spaces on the hard disk. This is known as fragmentation. Disk Defragmenter reorders the data.

Watch out
When you start to run Disk Defragmenter, you will be prompted for an Administrator password. Even if you are an administrator you will be asked for permission to continue.

Disk Defragmenter

Disk Defragmenter consolidates fragmented files on your computer's performance. How does Disk Defragmenter help?

Run on a schedul

Scheduled defragme

Last run: 03/10/2007

Next scheduled run: Never

✓ **Your file system performance is good**
You do not need to defragment at this time.

◯ **Analyzing disks...**
This may take a few minutes

Defragment now

---

3 You should analyse your hard disk for **fragmentation** once a month or after installing programs. To defragment your hard disk, you must be logged on as an Administrator and a minimum of 15 per cent free disk space is required to complete the task. Go to the **Start** menu and select **All Programs**, **Accessories**, then **System Tools**. Click on **Disk Defragmenter**. Windows then automatically analyses your disks. When completed, it reports what action, if any, needs to be undertaken. If prompted by the system, click on **Defragment now**.

4 Alternatively, you can set Disk Defragmenter to run on a scheduled basis. To do this, click on the **Start** button, **All Programs**, **Accessories**, **System Tools**, then on **Disk Defragmenter**. Select the option **Run on a** schedule (recommended). To change the frequency, day and time of the defragmenter schedule, click on **Modify schedule**. Select alternatives for each of the three options, by using the drop-down menus in each box.

Disk Defragmenter: Modify Schedule

Run disk defragmenter on this schedule:

How often: Weekly

What day: Wednesday

What time: 01:00

Disk Defragme

Disk De
perform

☑ Run on a schedule (recommended)

Run at 01:00 every Wednesday, starting 01/01/2005

Last run: 09/10/2007 14:29

Next scheduled run: 10/10/2007 01:00

✓ **Scheduled defragmentation is enabled**
Your disks will be defragmented at the scheduled time.

Modify schedule...

Defragment now

OK   C

Back up your work

To avoid losing important work in the event of a problem with your hard disk, it makes sense to back up your files. When you create a backup, Windows compresses your files and folders and copies them onto a storage disc. You can then update your backup files at regular intervals. This means you can restore your work if files become corrupt.

SEE ALSO...
- *Copy and move files* *p34*
- *Create your own shortcuts* *p41*

BEFORE YOU START... Make sure you have adequate storage space for backing up your work. It is best to use either a recordable CD (CD-R) or DVD (DVD-R).

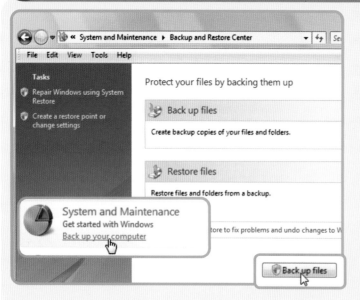

1 Windows Vista Home Premium edition includes the Windows Backup program. To start a backup, click on the **Start** button and then on **Control Panel**. Under 'System and Maintenance', click on **Back up your computer**. This will open the Backup and Restore Center. Now click on the **Back up files** button. When prompted for permission to continue, click on **Continue**.

2 Select where you want to save your backup and click on **Next**. In the next window, select the types of file that you would like to back up from the list. Note that the first backup you make will copy everything from your hard drive to the destination disc. Click on **Next**.

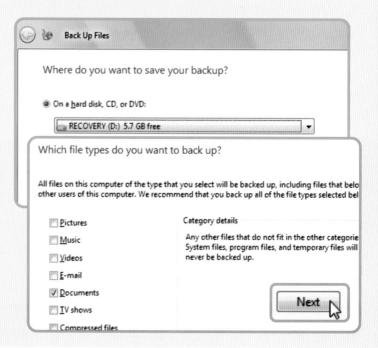

Expert advice
Always carefully label, date and number the discs you use for backing up. Store these discs (CDs, DVDs or external hard drive) in a secure place – a separate fireproof location is ideal.

Back Up Files

How often do you want to create a backup?

New files and files that have changed will be added to your backup according to the schedule you se below.

How often: Weekly

What day: Sunday

What time: 19:00

Because this is your first backup, Windows will create a new, full backup now.

Back Up Files

Backing up files

Copying files to D:\

To restore your data, launch Backup as in step 1 and click on **Restore files**. You can restore files from the latest backup or from an older set. Select an option and click on **Next**. Now, using the buttons on the right, click on **Add files** or **Add folders** and select the items to restore. If you're not sure of a file or folder name, click on **Search**, type part of the name into the box and click on **Search** to find it. When you have all the items to restore in your list, click on **Next**. Finally, select the location for your restored items and click on **Start restore**.

Restore files

Restore Files

What do you want to restore?

⦿ Files from the latest backup

○ Files from an older backup

Select the files and folders to restore

Name	In Folder	Date modified
Personal Finance	C:\Users\Tone\Docum...	24/07/2007 13:10
Business Records	C:\Users\Tone\Docum...	19/07/2007 19:19
HTDJAIV_Grabs	C:\Users\Tone\Desktop	10/10/2007 16:36

Other options:

Repair Window

See recently d

Learn how to r

Add files...

Add folders...

Start restore

3 In the next window you can set the frequency, day of the week and time of a scheduled data backup – make your selections using the drop-down menus. However, if this is your first backup, a message will inform you that a complete backup will be performed, irrespective of the options you chose. Click on **Save settings and start backup** to begin the backup process.

Computer viruses

Vista is much more secure than previous versions of Windows and it is therefore less likely that you will encounter a virus. However, you should still take the threat of viruses seriously as they can do a great deal of damage. Always be careful about the files you allow into your computer and use virus checking software to check for infected files before you open them.

SEE ALSO...
- Back up your work p48

VIRUSES EXPLAINED
Find out what viruses are, why they exist, how they spread and what you can do to avoid them.

What are viruses?
Viruses are programs or segments of code that run without your knowledge. They are usually disguised and may sit on your computer for some time before activating. This gives them a chance to replicate or spread to programs, files and other connected computers before being discovered. There are all kinds of viruses, with different capabilities and methods of attack.

What can they do to my computer?
Some viruses are relatively harmless – for instance, they may cause a message to appear on your screen for no apparent reason. But other viruses aim to damage files so that you may lose some of your work or, worse still, they may damage vital Windows files, so you have to reinstall your system.

Who creates viruses and why?
Viruses are deliberately programmed by people who set out to spread them to as many computers as possible. There are many reasons why they do this. They could have political and ideological motives: a virus can be a protest against a government or market dominance. Or it might be an ego trip for someone who wishes to prove themselves as smarter than the software engineers.

How could I catch a virus?
Like a cold, a computer virus has to be caught, so it has to get into your PC from an external source. Such sources include:
External drives: If you often use CD-ROMs, DVDs or other removable discs, you could unwittingly open an infected file. A friend could give you a virus without even realising it.
The Web: You should download files from reputable sites only. Legitimate Web sites should state that they use anti-virus software to check all downloadable files and programs.
E-mail: The most common way to catch a virus is via an e-mail attachment. An attachment is a self-contained data file sent with an e-mail. When an e-mail includes an attachment, a paperclip is displayed beside the e-mail details (see below). Typically, you need to click on the paperclip to open and view the attachment. Only open an attachment if you know the person who sent it and are sure that they intended to send you the file.

Close up
Not all CD-ROMs are a potential risk. Those from reputable software companies are unlikely to contain viruses. However, you should be cautious when using recordable or rewritable CDs created on another person's PC.

Watch out
E-mail is a popular vehicle for viruses but downloading an e-mail will not allow a virus to spread – you have to open the message or attachment. Unfortunately, most e-mail software automatically displays the contents of a message so, if you use e-mail, it is important to protect your system with anti-virus software.

TYPES OF VIRUS

Viruses take various forms and can attack your computer's files in different ways. Here are some of the main culprits.

File infector

This is a virus that attaches itself to program files. Program files are 'executable', which means that if you open the file, you launch a program. So if you don't open the file, the virus cannot run. Be suspicious of e-mail attachments or unverifiable downloads ending in '.exe', '.com', '.vbx' or '.bat', but also be aware that files created by programs such as Word and Excel could easily carry a macro virus. Windows will warn you about viruses when you start a download.

Boot sector virus

The boot sector contains files that tell your computer how to load the operating system each time you start up. If you insert a CD or DVD containing a boot sector virus into your computer, you will be able to read files on the disc without a problem. However, if you restart your PC with the CD still in the drive, your PC will access it, run the virus, and then may stop working. You should always avoid leaving a CD or DVD in the drive when you turn off your computer. Check your BIOS manual for information on boot sector virus protection.

Multipartite virus

Like file infectors, these viruses attach themselves to program files. When activated, they attack your hard drive's boot sector, so that the computer doesn't know how to find and load the operating system. This makes it impossible to start up your computer. Luckily, these viruses are hard to program and rare.

Macro virus

Some programs, such as Word and Excel, enable you to create macros, which are a series of instructions that you set up. Anyone with knowledge of the Visual Basic programming language can create a macro virus. If you open

a Word or Excel file containing a macro virus, it can spread to all your Word or Excel files. Macro viruses are not common these days and are easy to avoid as both Word and Excel display a box telling you macros are present when you open the file. Unless you're sure where they came from, click on the **Disable Macros** button.

Worm

A virus can replicate itself, but to move from computer to computer, the user has to pass on the infected file. Worms, on the other hand, can spread themselves. The famous worm trick is to e-mail itself to everyone in your Address Book. Computer networks are particularly vulnerable, as viruses can spread very quickly.

Trojan horse

These pretend to be harmless, even useful, applications. Then, when you least expect it, something nasty happens. Trojan horses are not classified as viruses because they cannot replicate themselves to infect other files on your computer.

Virus hoaxes

If you use e-mail, you are probably used to virus warnings. Unfortunately, it's hard to know when these are genuine and when they are just practical jokes. The danger of hoaxes is that you may start to ignore real warnings. Combat this by looking up the latest viruses on reputable Web sites, such as www.mcafee.com and www.symantec.com.

I Love You

In the year 2000, the infamous worm 'I Love You' brought computers and networks to a halt all over the world. It arrived as an e-mail file attachment called 'LOVE-LETTER-FOR-YOU.TEXT.vbs'. When the recipient opened the file, it read through the Address Book on that person's computer and forwarded itself to all the e-mail addresses it had read. Although it only affected Microsoft Outlook and Outlook Express, the 'I Love You' worm managed to spread around the world in a matter of hours, damaging data on millions of PCs and blocking up company networks with unwanted e-mails. The culprit was a young programmer in the Far East.

AVOIDING VIRUSES

There are many ways to safeguard your computer from being infected with a disruptive virus.

Anti-virus programs

These programs protect you against thousands of known viruses. The two best-known applications are McAfee Security Center and Norton AntiVirus from Symantec.

You can set up your anti-virus program to run in the background, so that it keeps regular checks on your computer and vets all incoming e-mails and external discs, such as CDs and DVDs.

Alternatively, you can run a virus check manually and choose exactly which drive and which files you want it to scan. Generally, the first place to look is the C: drive, where your operating system files are saved.

You've found a virus

When you run a virus scan, a log file documents the results. You can check this file at any time.

If your anti-virus program finds an infected file, you need to decide what to do with it. The file can be moved to a separate folder, deleted, or noted and left. Your program may be able to clean the file so that you can carry on using it. However, the safest option is to quarantine it.

Free updates

New viruses appear all the time, which is why the Web support provided by your software manufacturer is vital. Anti-virus programmers spend their working lives looking for viruses and creating fixes. Often you never hear about a virus because a fix is made before it spreads. Both McAfee and Symantec provide the latest anti-virus lists and software as automatic updates, similar to Windows Update. You can also sign up for e-mail newsletters, keeping you up to date on any new viruses for which fixes have not yet been created.

Better safe than sorry

Anti-virus software wards off most viruses, but there are additional steps you can take to keep your PC clean:

1 Keeping all of your software up to date helps to beat hackers. Microsoft sometimes issues patches for program loopholes on its Web site. You should also check your other software manufacturers' Web sites regularly for updates and patches.

2 Back up your hard drive regularly (see page 48) and make sure you have the original discs for your programs and operating system.

If a virus infects your computer and you lose everything, you'll need to reinstall the software and all your data.

3 If you don't have the latest version of your anti-virus software, try an on-line virus-scanning service, such as HouseCall from Trend Micro (http.housecall.trendmicro.com/uk/).

4 Beware of e-mail attachments, even if they are from a friend. Avoid downloadable newsgroup files, and only download files from reputable Web sites.

5 Set up safety settings on your Web browser. For instance, you can choose to be prompted should you start to download a file by mistake. If you are using Internet Explorer, click on the **Tools** menu and select **Internet Options** and then the **Security** tab. Click on the **Custom Level** or **Default Level** buttons to adjust your settings, click on **OK**, and then on **OK** again.

Windows Defender

Vista comes with Windows Defender, a piece of anti-spyware software designed to detect and alert you when potentially malicious software is trying to install itself on your computer. When you use Windows Defender, it is important to have up-to-date definitions (a log of potential software threats). To help keep your definitions up to date, Windows Defender works with Windows Update to automatically install new definitions as they are released. To run Windows Defender, click on the **Start** button, **All Programs**, **Windows Defender** and then on **Scan**. You can schedule Windows Defender to run automatically. Click on **Tools**, **Options** and then, using the drop-down lists, set your automatic scanning preferences.

Word

Explore the program

Many people use Word more frequently than other programs. Although Word is designed to be intuitive, you will be able to use it more confidently and efficiently if you first take time to get to know the functions in the main document window. This will provide you with a better understanding of the many powerful features on offer.

SEE ALSO...
- *What is Word?* *p13*
- *Entering text* *p58*

BEFORE YOU START
You may have a shortcut for accessing Word on your computer Desktop.

Look out for a 'Word' icon, with a small arrow in the bottom left-hand corner. Double-click on this to run Word.

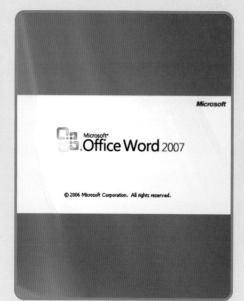

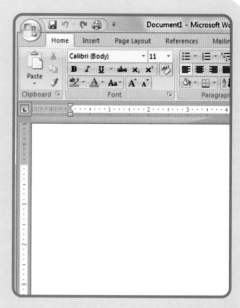

2 As the program opens, you will see a title window appear briefly. This tells you which version of Word you are using. After a few seconds this window disappears and the program continues to load.

1 If you don't have a Desktop shortcut to Word, click on the **Start** button, move the pointer to **All Programs** and select **Microsoft Office**. Click on **Microsoft Office Word 2007** to run the program. Once you have used Word, the program will appear as an item in your Start menu (see above) for quick and easy access.

3 A blank Word document will appear on screen, into which you can start typing text. However, before you do this it is best to become acquainted with the window and the tools that you might want to use to manipulate your text.

THE DOCUMENT WINDOW

Commands for manipulating text and documents are displayed as buttons on the Ribbon and are grouped by similar functions. These are all organised within tabs. There are often different ways of accessing the same command.

Office button
Gives access to options for opening, printing and saving documents.

Command tabs
Click on a tab to access a range of related commands.

Group
Similar functions are organised within a group.

Rulers
Shows you the width of your text area and any indents or tabs you have set. Clicking and sliding the small tabs along the ruler changes the setting. The vertical ruler shows your top and bottom print margins.

Status bar
Shows the current status of your document. It tells you which page you are viewing and how many pages your document contains. It displays the number of words in the document, the spell check status and in what language dictionary was used.

Quick Access Toolbar
These buttons activate common commands such as Save and Print.

Minimize button
Click here to reduce your document to a named button on the Taskbar at the bottom of the screen (see 'Minimized' button, below).

Maximize/Restore button
This button enlarges the window, so it fills the screen. After maximising, the button looks like two overlapping boxes. Click again to restore the window to its previous size.

Close button
The red button with a white cross closes the program.

Scroll bars
Use the up and down arrows to scroll up and down your document. You can also click and drag the grey block up or down to move quickly through multiple-page documents

Cursor
The flashing cursor, or 'insertion point', appears at the start of a new document to show you where text will be inserted

Double arrows buttons
Click here to view the previous page (up arrows) or the following page (down arrows)

Taskbar
Contains the Start button and many useful shortcuts to your programs and settings.

'Minimized' button
Shows which other programs/documents are currently open. Here, 'Corel Paint Shop Pro' has been minimised. Click on the button to restore the program or document.

View buttons
Click on these to change the way your document is displayed, such as a print preview or Web layout format.

Zoom level
Click and drag the slider to increase or decrease the viewing level.

COMMAND TABS

All the tasks you could want to perform in Word are displayed within groups. These are all found on the Ribbon within the different tabs.

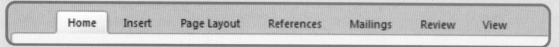

Before you start using Word, it's a good idea to click on each tab to familiarise yourself with the options it displays. Most commands have icons illustrating their function.

The Home tab

This gives you access to basic text editing and formatting functions, such as copying and pasting items and changing fonts.

The Insert tab

This allows you to add extra pages to your document and insert tables, illustrations and symbols.

The Page Layout tab

This gives you options for laying out your documents.

The References tab

Here you can access special features to enhance your documents, such as footnotes, a table of contents, cross-references, a bibliography, captions, and an index.

Expert advice

If you aren't sure what all the icons on your PC mean, go to the **Office** button and select **Word Options** then **Popular**. In the 'Top options for working with Word' section, click on the drop-down arrow next to 'ScreenTip style' and select **Show feature descriptions in ScreenTips**. Now, whenever you hover the mouse pointer over an icon the ScreenTip will tell you what it does and what the keyboard shortcut is, if there is one.

Close up

Click on the arrow, known as a dialogue box launcher, at the bottom right of a 'group' to view a dialogue box of commands for that group.

The Mailings tab

This gives you access to all the Mail Merge functions.

The Review tab

This lets you add comments to documents and track changes made by others to your documents.

The View tab

Here you can choose how documents are displayed and whether elements such as the ruler and gridlines are shown or hidden.

CONTEXTUAL TABS

The tabs displayed on the Ribbon change depending on the action you are performing. For example, when you are editing a table the Table Tools tab is displayed and when a graphic image is selected the Drawing Tools tab appears, displaying additional commands to assist you.

The Mini Toolbar

Whenever you have text selected the Mini Toolbar will appear close by. It gives immediate access to the most commonly used text formatting options.

Highlight a piece of text and with the mouse pointer positioned over the highlighted area, slowly move the mouse upwards. The Mini Toolbar will gradually appear over the highlighted area. Click on one of the options to change your text.

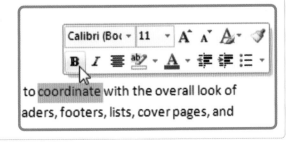

Entering text

Type in your text and you will see it appear on the page of the open document. You do not have to press the 'Return' key at the end of each line, as the text will automatically flow on to the next line. It doesn't matter if you make mistakes, as you can edit your work at any point, deleting text or moving it around the page.

SEE ALSO...
- *What is Word?* *p13*
- *Explore the program* *p54*

BEFORE YOU START
*Open a new blank document by clicking on the **Office** button and then on **New.*** *In the New Document dialogue box, click on **Blank Document** and then on the **Create** button.*

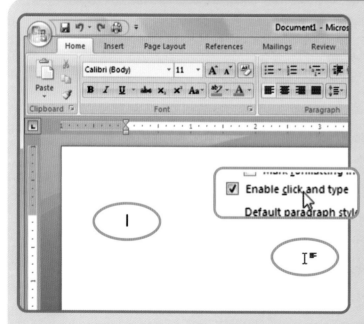

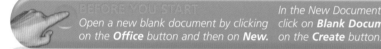

1 When you open any document the cursor appears at the start of the first page. In Print Layout view, with 'Enable click and type' ticked in 'Word Options', place the cursor where you want to type. The pointer shape shows the format of the text, double-click and then start typing your text.

2 In Word, text flows or 'wraps' automatically onto the next line when you reach the right-hand margin. You only need to press the Return key to start a new paragraph, or end a line early, or when making a list. Click the **Show/Hide** button in the 'Paragraph' group to reveal or hide non-printing characters, such as returns and spaces.

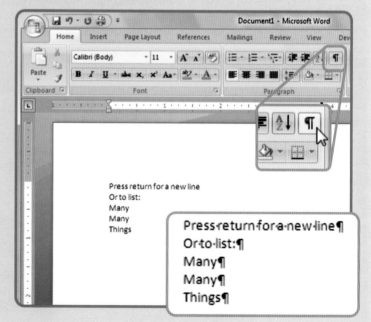

Expert advice
The keys on your computer's keyboard have different functions and different names. Some, such as the 'Shift' key, need to be held down while you press another key. Others, such as the 'Caps Lock' key, are known as toggle switches: press them once and they are switched on; press them again and they are switched off. The function keys (F1 to F12) are above the standard letter and number keys. These are used for keyboard commands.

Close up
Word can check spelling and grammar for you. A wavy red line appears under misspelt or unrecognisable words. Text that it thinks is grammatically incorrect is marked by a wavy green line.

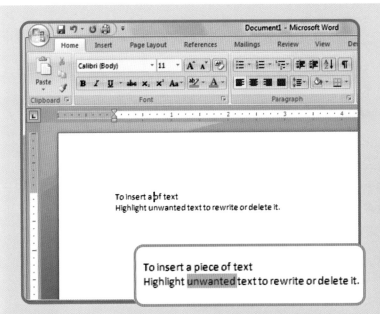

4 To type a capital letter, hold down the **Shift** key and press the letter key. Shift also causes the upper symbol on a key with two symbols, to be typed. For example, press **Shift + 5** to type '%'. If you want to type a series of capital letters, press the **Caps Lock** key. A green light on the right of your keyboard reminds you that the lock is on. To unlock it, press **Caps Lock** once more.

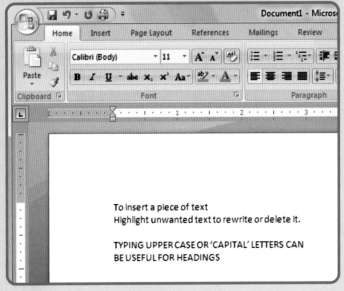

3 To insert words between existing text, move your cursor to the desired position, click and type. Use the **Backspace** key to delete errors to the left of the cursor. You can also delete text by clicking and dragging the mouse pointer over text to highlight it, then pressing the **Backspace** or the **Delete** key. Alternatively, you can highlight the text and type straight over it.

Save your work

Any new document should be saved as soon as possible after creating it, and you should continue to save any changes at regular intervals. This is important because sometimes computers crash, which means that your screen freezes and you have to exit the program without saving your files. So, if you don't save regularly, you run the risk of losing hours of work.

SEE ALSO...

● *Entering text p58*

BEFORE YOU START
To save a document for the first time, click on the **Office** button and choose **Save**. Alternatively, you can click the **Save** button on the Quick Access Toolbar, or use the keyboard shortcut **Ctrl + S**.

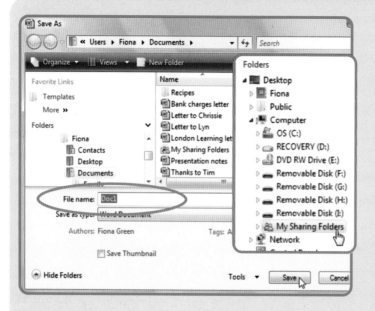

2 Your Documents folder is a good place to store your work. However, it also makes sense to organise your files into subfolders – for instance, one folder for all your bank letters, another for your Web site, or a folder for each family member. If you want a new folder, click the **New Folder** icon and type in a name. To select and open the folder you wish to save into, double-click on it.

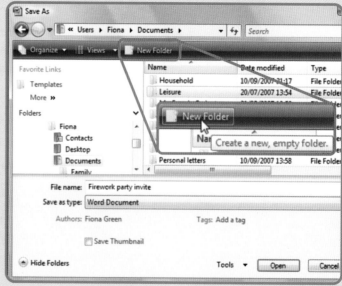

1 The first time you save a document, the Save As dialogue box opens. You will need to name your document and choose where to save it. A suggested name, usually the first line, is highlighted in the 'File name' panel. Type a name over it.
    Word prompts you to save in your Documents folder. Click on the arrow to the right of the panel if you want to choose a different location.

Expert advice
To save another version of a document go to the **Start** button and select **Save As.** You can then give the version a new name or choose to store it in an alternative location. This offers a quick and easy method for creating a backup file in another folder or on another disk, or for saving different versions of a file.

Bright idea
Create a template so you don't have to restyle your letters each time. Set up a page the way you want and save it. In the 'Save as type' panel, select Word Template. *Next time you create a new document, you can choose your template from the New dialogue box.*

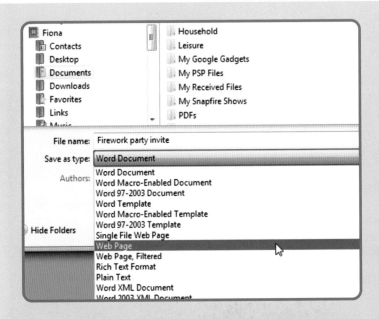

3 Choose how to save your file in the 'Save as type' panel. Most of the time you will save as a 'Word Document'. If you're creating a Web site, save your file as a 'Web Page'. 'Rich Text Format' retains your document setup, but can be opened by many other programs. 'Plain Text' saves files as text with no styling or formatting, but the text can then be read in almost any program.

4 When you are happy with your options, click on the **Save** button. The file name in the pale grey Title bar at the top of the window changes from 'Document1', for example, to the name you have given it. As you work, you need to keep saving your changes. The quickest way is to click the 'Save' icon on the Quick Access Toolbar, top left, or press **Ctrl + S.**

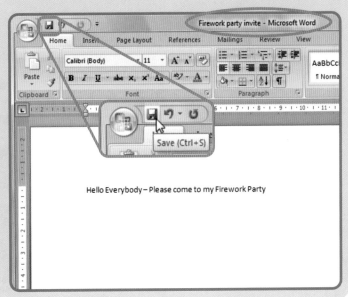

Choose and size a font

The appearance of any document can be changed dramatically through the use of different fonts, or 'typefaces', and by making text such as headings a different size. With Word, you even have the ability to use many different fonts and sizes on any page to create exactly the overall effect that you are looking for.

SEE ALSO...
- *Style and colour text* p64
- *Format a document* p68

BEFORE YOU START
To change text to a different font, highlight the text that you want to change. You can then choose to make individual changes quickly, or to make several changes at once.

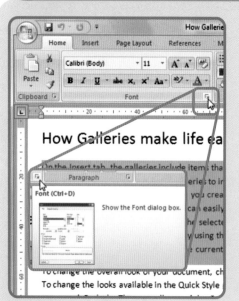

1 When you want to make several changes to your text – to alter font, size and style all at once, for example – it is quicker to do everything at the same time using the Font dialogue box. Click on the Font dialogue box launcher to open the dialogue box.

2 The default font for the template you are using is highlighted in the 'Font' panel. A line of your own text is shown in this default font in the 'Preview' pane at the bottom.

To view the text in a different font, scroll down the list in the 'Font' panel. Select a font name and look again in the 'Preview' pane to see your text displayed in the selected font.

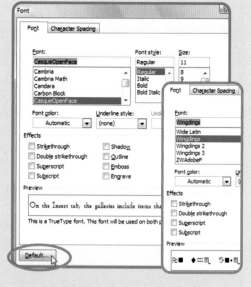

3 Scroll through, select and view different typefaces (some of them have symbols, not letters). Click on **OK** to confirm your selection. To change the default font for a template you are using, select a font and click on the **Default** button, then on **OK.** This changes the document and the template.

Serif or sans-serif

Two common fonts in use today are 'Times New Roman' and 'Arial'. 'Times New Roman' was developed as a typeface for *The Times* newspaper and is a serif font. This means that there are short, fine lines at the ends of the strokes of each character – this was thought to lead the eye smoothly from one letter to the next. 'Arial' was developed later, and is a sans-serif (without serif) font. Research has shown that a serif font is generally more readable when used in long documents, but that a sans-serif font is clearer for anyone who is partially sighted.

Times New Roman
Arial

Key word
The height of a font is measured in points, and there are precisely 72 points to an inch (2.5cm). A standard 12-point font measures one-sixth of an inch (4mm) in height on the page.

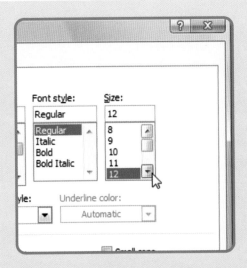

4 Using the arrows, scroll and select a font size from the list. If the size you want is not there, click on the box and type a figure, then press **Return** and your text will change.

   The largest standard font size is 72 point. If you need a bigger size, try using WordArt. There are also various text effects to choose from, including shadows and embossed type.

5 You can make individual changes to text more quickly by using the formatting buttons on the Ribbon. To alter the font, highlight your text and click on the down arrow to the right of the 'Font' panel. A drop-down list gives all the fonts available, with their names displayed in the associated typeface.

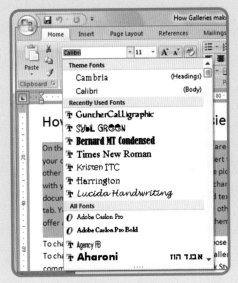

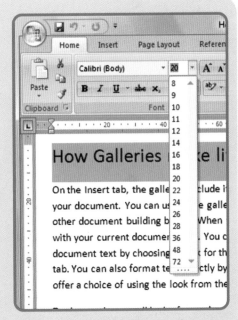

6 For quick changes to the size of an item of text, highlight it, then click on the down arrow to the right of the 'Font Size' box found in the 'Font' group. A drop-down menu lists point sizes. Click on one to select it.

Style and colour text

Changing the style of your text is a sure way to alter the look of a document and draw the reader's attention to specific points that you wish to make. You can add emphasis and different styles to your characters by using some of the specific enhancements, such as italics, or by underlining and colouring parts of your text.

SEE ALSO...
- *Choose and size a font p62*
- *Format a paragraph p70*

BEFORE YOU START
Highlight the text you want to make changes to, and click on the Font dialogue box launcher in the 'Font' group. Use this box to make several different changes to a piece of text.

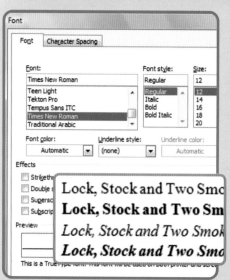

1 Select the style you wish to use in the 'Font style' panel. For emphasis, choose to embolden (Bold) or italicise (Italic) headings, rather than underlining them. Italicised text can look smaller than regular text, so you might want to embolden it, too. View changes in the 'Preview' pane.

2 To alter the colour of your selected text, click on the arrow by the 'Font color' panel. Select a colour by clicking on one of the square colour buttons. In the 'Preview' pane, you will see your coloured text.

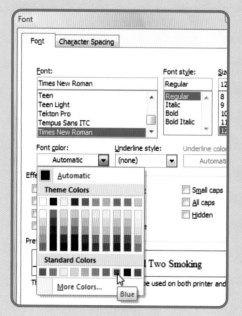

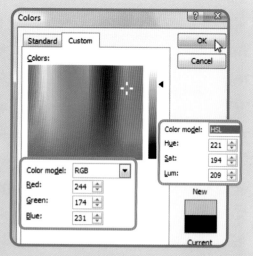

3 For a wider range of colours, click on **More Colors**. Select the **Standard** tab or the **Custom** tab for further choices. Click on a colour and it appears in the smaller 'New' pane.
   Under the 'Custom' tab, you can customise the colour via the 'Color model' options for RGB (Red, Green, Blue) and HSL (Hue, Saturation, Luminescence). Click on **OK** to finish.

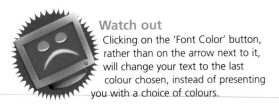

Bright idea
'Hidden' text, which is one of the 'Effects' options, allows you to make notes in your document which will show on the computer screen but will not print out.

5 Click on the box of your choice in the 'Effects' section to select a further style. 'Superscript' is used for above-the-line text items like dates (16th), while 'Subscript' is for below-the-line items like 'H_2O'. Visual effects such as 'Emboss' and 'Engrave' can look faint in print depending on their colour.

Strikethrough	Lock, Stock and Two Smok
Double Strikethrough	Lock, Stock and Two Smok
Superscript	Lock, Stock and Two Smokin
Subscript	Lock, Stock and Two Smokin
Shadow	Lock, Stock and Two Smok
Outline	Lock, Stock and Two Smok
Emboss	Lock, Stock and Two Smok
Engrave	Lock, Stock and Two Smok
Small Caps	LOCK, STOCK AND TWO SM
All Caps	LOCK, STOCK AND TWO
Hidden	

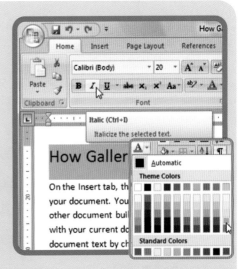

4 Click on the arrow beside 'Underline style' for a drop-down list of line styles. Use the scroll bar to move up and down. Click on a style to select it, then click on the arrow beside 'Underline color' to select a colour for the line.

6 If you want to use only one of these functions, it is quicker to use the button icons in the 'Font' group. You can change the font colour, as well as embolden, italicise and underline selected text. However, these buttons have limited functions. For example, you cannot underline in colour, nor can you access all the 'Effects' in the Font dialogue box.

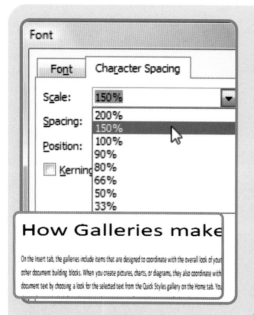

8 Imagine you have typed a heading, or your address, at the top of a page or column. You have centred the text, but the letters look too tightly squeezed together – you want to stretch them across without altering the font size. Click on the down arrow in the 'Spacing' box and select **Expanded** and use the 'By' box to define an amount. Select **Condensed** to do the opposite.

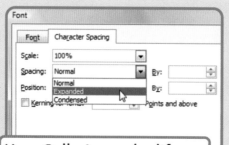

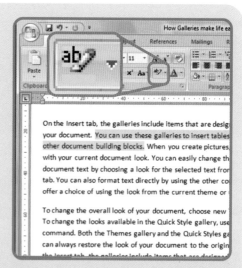

7 In the Font dialogue box, click on the **Character Spacing** tab. If you have different font sizes within your selected text, and you want to scale the size of the text up or down without altering the font sizes, select a percentage from the 'Scale' box.

9 If you need to, you can emphasise a portion of your text to make it appear as if it has been marked by a highlighter pen. First, using your mouse, click and drag through the relevant text. Then in the 'Font' group click on the text highlighter button. If you want to highlight text in a different colour, click on the arrow to the right of the button, and make your selection.

Inserting text breaks

Sometimes you'll want to start a new page, column or section before you have filled the last one with text. You might do this by pressing the 'Return' key repeatedly, but Word has a quicker way of creating breaks in text. You'll also have more control over the look and shape of your work, as you can reformat the text in each section to make it easier to read.

SEE ALSO...
- *Format a document p68*
- *Using columns and bullets   p72*

BREAKING UP TEXT

To break your text in a particular place, you need to insert a permanent break, which will remain unaffected by Word's automatic pagination.

Position the cursor in your document where you wish to make the break. You can create a break before you type any more text, or you can add breaks after you've typed your document. Go to

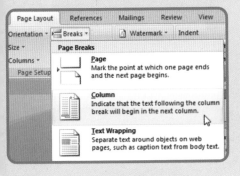

the **Insert** tab and select **Page Break** from the 'Pages' group. This will now move text from this point onto a new page. No matter how you alter the document, this text will always start at the top of a new page.

Break types

If you want a column to end before it reaches the bottom of the page, click on the **Page Layout** tab and select **Breaks** from the 'Page Setup' group. Then click on **Column**.

Select the **Text Wrapping** break option to force text to the beginning of a new line.

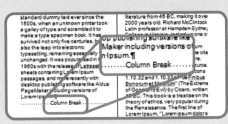

Section break types

If you want to format a part of your document differently on a separate page, select the section break option **Next page**. Now you can set text on that page over a different number of columns, or make it landscape (horizontal) while the rest of your document is portrait (vertical). If you want to incorporate a different layout within the same page, select **Continuous**. If you have created a document with facing pages, like a book, choose **Odd page** or **Even page** to start a new section on the next odd or even-numbered page.

Deleting breaks

If you no longer want a break, double-click the break to select it, then press the **Delete** key. You can also position your cursor after the break and press **Backspace** to delete it. If you can't see the dotted line break on your screen, click on the **Show/Hide** button in the 'Paragraph' group on the **Home** tab.

Bright idea
A quick way to insert a Page break is to hold down the Ctrl key and press the Return key.

Watch out
It is best not to create a page break by pressing the 'Return' key continuously until you reach a new page. Your text is fluid and will move up or down as you add or delete text later. The result is much more time consuming than using Word's built-in Break feature.

Format a document

The overall appearance of a document is determined by the formatting characteristics set up within the template in which you open it. You may want to add a new heading or items such as page numbers. If a pre-set heading is not quite perfect, you can modify it. If you work on many documents of the same type, you may even want to create your own style and save it as a template.

SEE ALSO...
- *Choose and size a font* p62
- *Format a paragraph* p70

BEFORE YOU START
Templates for document formats are divided into various styled paragraph and character items. Make sure that you are happy with the style options for the template you select.

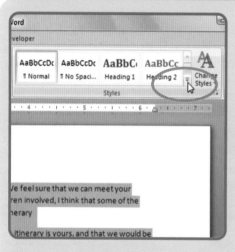

1 Highlight your text. With the Home tab selected, click on the down-pointing arrow in the 'Styles' group. A drop-down list displays styles available for the current document.

Hover you mouse pointer over any of the pre-set paragraph styles and your highlighted text will be displayed in that style. Move your mouse pointer away to revert to the original style. Click on a particular style to select it permanently.

2 Alternatively, click on the dialogue box launcher on the right of the 'Styles' group to view the 'Styles' pane, which lists additional pre-set styles. Hover the pointer over a style to check its details – if you want to use it click on its name to select it.

Click on the arrow on the right of the 'Show' panel for formatting and style options. For example, choose 'All styles' to view the available formatting styles.

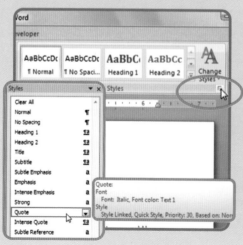

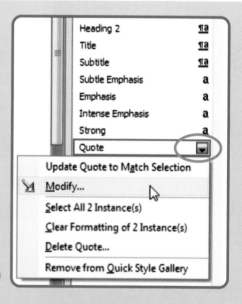

3 Styles are defined as either paragraph ('¶'), character(s) ('a') or both ('¶a'), to show whether they apply to a paragraph or words.

To alter a style, select it in the 'Styles' pane and when the icon to its right changes to a down arrow, click on it to reveal a list of options. Click on **Modify**.

Themes

You can style text using 'themes' which will give an integrated look to your document, ensuring that fonts, colours and related graphics, such as 'bullets', all work well together. To utilise this option, click on the **Page Layout** tab and select **Themes**. Browse through the themes in the gallery and hover your mouse pointer over an item to view your document in that theme.

Watch out

If you save changes to the original template, you can end up with a whole mixture of muddled styles. It is better to save new or modified styles as a new template, giving it a name you will recognise. To do this, click on the **Office** button, then **Save As** and select **Word Template** in the 'Save as type' panel.

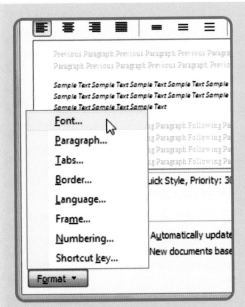

4 Click on the **Format** button to access a drop-down menu. Select and change any style details by clicking on each heading to open the appropriate dialogue box.

You can change the font and size, paragraphing, indents and so on.

5 Select 'New documents based on this template' only if you wish to use the modified style in new documents based on this template. Select 'Automatically update' to update all previous instances of that style in your document. Click on **OK** to modify the formatting for the selected paragraph and to return to the document.

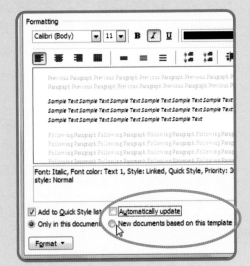

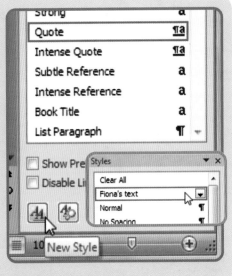

6 Click on the **New Style** button at the bottom of the 'Styles' pane to create a new style. Name it and modify items, selecting and defining those you need. You can add to the list at any time. Use the new styles in your document and save a version of the document as a template which you can use for similar documents.

Format a paragraph

Just as you can easily change the look of your entire document, so you can also change the layout, or 'format', of individual sections within it. Quoted text can be indented, either from the left or from both sides, while hanging indents can give a traditional look to your work. You can also prevent a single line straying on to the next page, or being left behind.

SEE ALSO...
● *Format a document* p68
● *Using tabs* p74

BEFORE YOU START
Highlight several paragraphs or click anywhere in a single paragraph to *select it. Click on the dialogue box launcher in the 'Paragraph' group, then on the **Indents and Spacing** tab.*

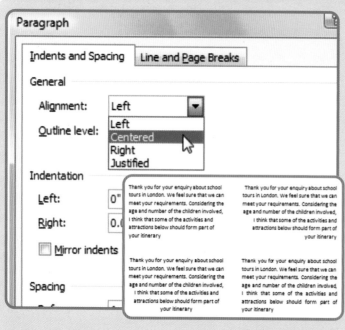

1 In the 'Alignment' panel, **Left** is already selected by default, so your text is lined up to the left side of the page. Click on the arrow to the right to select

'Centered' (text is centred on the page), 'Right' (to make it line up to the right side of the page), or 'Justified' (to stretch and align the text so that it is straight on both sides).

2 Under 'Indentation', select the 'Left' or 'Right' panel and scroll down to set how far in from the left or right edge of the page to place the text. This is good for indenting quotes.

Click in the 'Special' panel and select **First line**. Click on **By** to determine how far in from the main body of the paragraph the first line will be set. Select **Hanging** to indent all lines in a paragraph except for the first.

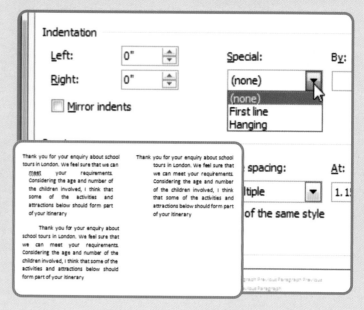

Ribbon shortcuts

You can also set the alignment by clicking on the alignment buttons in the 'Paragraph' group.

Paragraph indents can be changed by using the small 'Indent' markers at either end of the ruler at the top of the screen. Let your mouse hover over them. 'ScreenTips' show four types on the left: 'First Line', 'Left Margin', 'Hanging Indent', and 'Left Indent'.

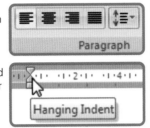

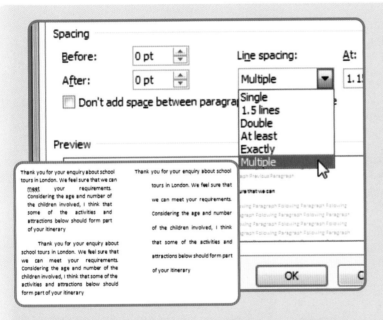

4 Click on the **Line and Page Breaks** tab. The 'Widow/Orphan control' option stops the last line of a paragraph appearing by itself at the top of the following page, or the first line being left on its own at the bottom of the previous page. You can also fine-tune paragraph breaks and opt to remove line numbers, or to turn off automatic hyphenation of words in this tab.

3 Select the 'Before' and 'After' panels to specify how much space will run before and after paragraphs in the selected text. Click in the 'Line spacing' panel to alter the spacing between lines within the paragraph. Letters are usually 'single' spaced, while typing draft documents in 'double spacing' leaves room for corrections. You can also set an exact amount of space or multiple lines.

Using columns and bullets

O ne very effective way of changing the appearance of your document is to put your text in columns. Try this with documents such as newsletters as it makes large amounts of text much easier to read. Alternatively, adding bullet points will help to display lists in a more accessible and logical way, while improving the overall look of your document.

SEE ALSO...

- *Format a document* p68
- *Using tabs* p74

BEFORE YOU START *Although you can format text into columns after you have finished typing, it is sensible to set the number of columns first, so you have a rough idea of how your pages will look.*

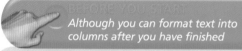

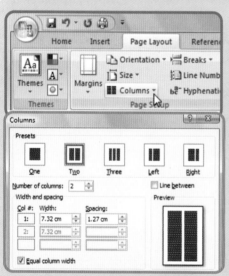

1 In the Page Layout tab, click on **Columns** in the 'Page Setup' group, then on **More Columns**. In the dialogue box, select the number of columns, either by choosing one of the presets or by typing the number into the panel. Then, either tick 'Equal column width' for evenly spaced columns, or specify each column width individually.

2 Your column format will apply to the whole of the document, unless you specify otherwise. If, for example, you need a heading, enter this first, leave a few line spaces and then set up your column format. In the dialogue box, make sure you have selected **This point forward** in the 'Apply to' panel. The 'line between' option allows you to put a visible line between your columns. Click on **OK** when your formatting is complete.

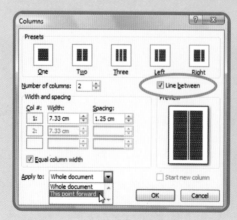

3 The cursor appears in your first column for you to begin typing. When the first column is full, your text will run straight into the next one. To force text over into the next column, position your cursor where you want the break, click on the **Page Layout** tab, select **Breaks** from the 'Page Setup' group and then click on **Column**.

Use your ruler

Column width can be altered quickly using the ruler at the top of the page. Blue areas relate to margins between the columns. Click the edge of a column and drag it to the required size. If you select equal column width, all columns will alter to match. You can change page margins in the same way.

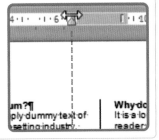

Numbered lists

These can be created, customised and new styles defined, using the processes explained in steps 1 and 2 below. To start using the 'Numbering' features click on the down arrow to the right of the 'Numbering' icon in the 'Paragraph' group.

---

1 To give your text added emphasis, use bullet points. Click on the down arrow to the right of the 'bullet' icon in the 'Paragraph' group. The dialogue box that appears gives you a range of bullet point styles to choose from. Click to select a style of bullet in the 'Bullet Library', then click on **OK**. Each time you press **Return** in your text, a new bullet will be added.

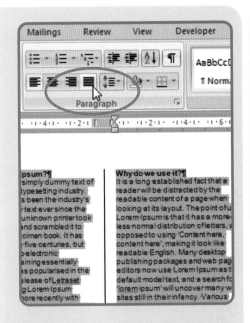

4 Your text can then be styled and formatted in the normal way. To avoid awkward line ends in narrow columns, it is a good idea to justify your text. This will give it a more professional look. Highlight the text and click on the **Justify** icon in the 'Paragraph' group.

2 To create your own bulleted style, click on **Define New Bullet**, at the bottom of the 'Bullet Library'. In the dialogue box click on the **Symbol** button to display characters from the 'Symbol' font. Select a character, then click on **OK**. Choose an option from the 'Alignment' panel, and check your selections in the 'Preview' pane. When finished, click on **OK**. Your new bullet style now appears in the library.

Using tabs

The 'Tab' feature allows you to align your text – or 'tabulate' it. This is a quick way of moving words across the page, rather than pressing the spacebar repeatedly. While you would create a table to organise lots of information into columns and rows, tabs are a handy way of tidying up a letter, an invoice, or a few simple columns of information.

SEE ALSO...

● *Using columns and bullets* *p72*

BEFORE YOU START
When you are working with tabs, it is a good idea to have the tabs showing.

*Click on the **Show/Hide** button in the 'Paragraph' group to reveal them, if they are not already visible.*

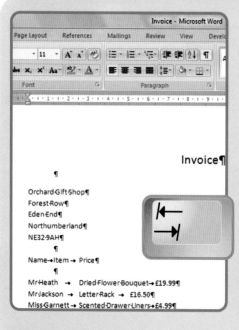

1 Microsoft Word opens with tabs set at the default position of 0.5 inches or metric equivalent. Pressing the **Tab** key on your keyboard causes the cursor to jump along the line to these preset positions.

2 To set your own tabs instead of using the defaults, highlight the document or the section to which tabs should apply. Click on the dialogue box launcher in the 'Paragraph' group and, with the Indents and Spacing tab selected, click on **Tabs**. Enter the position of your first tab in the 'Tab stop position' panel. Add more tabs, clicking on **Set** after each one.

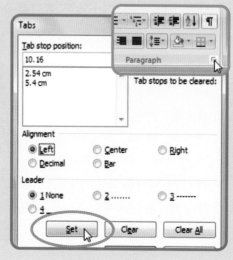

3 The Tabs dialogue box also allows you to change the alignment of your tabs. The default setting is aligned to the left, but you can align the tabs to the middle ('Center') of the text or to the right.

Tab shortcut

A quick way to set your tabs is by using the ruler at the top of the page. Highlight your text. Then, simply by clicking on the ruler at the required tab position, a left-aligned tab will be set. To change the alignment, click on the top left-hand corner to change the icon from left to centre or right-aligned tabs.

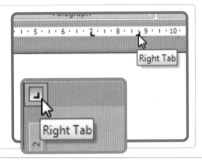

Bright idea
If you prefer to work in inches go to the Tools *menu and select* Options*. Select the* General *tab and look under 'Measurement units' for a drop-down list that offers you a choice of units. Select* Inches *then click on* OK*.*

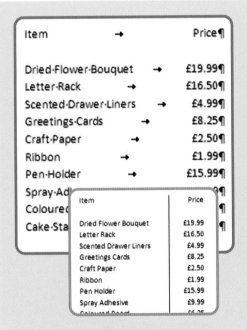

5 A further option allows you to fill in the space between your tabs with a type of line called a leader. The default setting is 'none', but you can select from the options beneath 'Leader' to insert dots, a broken line or a solid line. These options work especially well when you are displaying columns of figures.

4 If your tabulated text includes figures, select the 'Decimal' alignment button. This aligns all your numbers at the decimal point. Selecting 'Bar' gives you a vertical dividing line at the position of the tab.

6 The bottom of the Tabs dialogue box has a number of buttons. To delete a tab you've set, select it and click on **Clear**. Click on **Clear All** to automatically remove all of your tabs.
When you're happy with your settings, click on **OK** to return to your document.

Templates

Every time you create a new document in Word 2007, you are offered the 'Blank Document' template, which is an empty document with a pre-defined layout. However, there are a variety of other templates available, some already installed on your system and numerous others available from the Microsoft Office Online collection.

SEE ALSO...
- *Choose and size a font p62*
- *Format a document p68*

BEFORE YOU START
Office 2007 has a huge list of ready made templates which you can use as a base and adapt for your requirements. In this project, we are creating a formal letter.

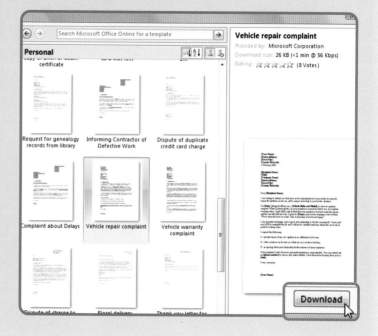

1 Click on the **Office** button, then on **New**. This opens the New Document pane. Under the 'Microsoft Office Online' section of the pane on the left, scroll down the list to find the category that you are looking for, here 'Letters'. Click on **Letters**, then from the pane on the right, click on **Personal**.

2 In the middle panel you will now see a selection of thumbnail images of different types of pre-formed letter templates. Click on an image to preview a larger version in the right panel. Select a style, in this case 'Vehicle repair complaint', and click on **Download**.

That's amazing!
You can create your own templates to re-use as often as you wish. To save a document as a template, click on the **Office** button, then **Save As**. Name your file. In the 'Save as type' panel, select **Word Template**. Your new template will be added to the templates available when you create a new document.

Watch out
Many of the templates provided by Word were created specifically for American users. This means that they may not always be appropriate in the UK.

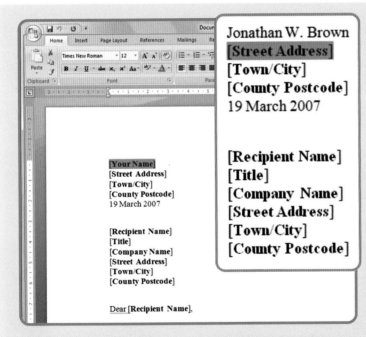

3 Your downloaded letter will have bracketed bold 'Prompt' areas within it. Click inside the brackets to highlight the prompt, and type your own details where appropriate. Other areas of the letter will need modifying, so highlight these as you go through and insert your own details. Delete any prompts that are not appropriate.

4 Now you can style and personalise your letter. For example, highlight your name and address at the top of the letter, then go to the **Home** tab and click on the Font dialogue box launcher. Select a font, style and size, clicking on any of interest to view them in the Preview window. Make your selection then click on **OK**.

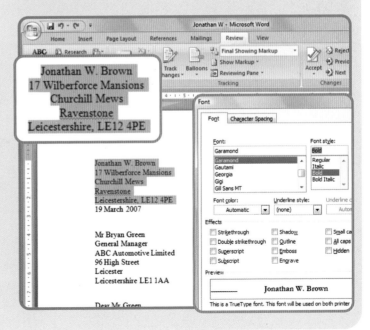

Cut, copy and paste

Word enables you to reorganise a document in no time by taking text, or images, from one area and placing them in another – this is called 'cutting and pasting'. If text needs to be repeated, you can copy it, leaving the original intact. You can then paste the text as many times as you like, wherever you like, without the need to type it all again.

SEE ALSO...
- *Templates p76*
- *Add a picture p84*

BEFORE YOU START
With a document open, highlight the item you want to copy. This can be a word, a phrase, a paragraph, a whole page, even several pages, or an illustration, such as a piece of ClipArt.

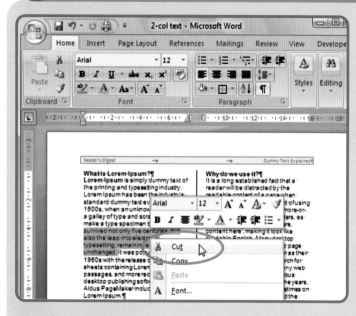

2 Right-click and choose **Paste** from the drop-down menu. Your text appears in the new location. You may need to check and readjust the spacing in your document. To move text just a short distance, highlight it, then drag and drop it on the page wherever you wish.

1 Right-click on the highlighted text and select either **Cut** or **Copy** from the drop-down menu. Text is stored on the computer's Clipboard, waiting to be used. If you are unsure of the effect of any changes, use 'Copy' then go back and delete unwanted text after pasting. Click in the document so that the insertion point appears where you want to paste the text.

Shortcuts

The 'Cut', 'Copy' and 'Paste' buttons in the 'Clipboard' group of the Home tab offer a speedy way to reorganise your work. Keyboard shortcuts for these commands are respectively, **Ctrl + X**, **Ctrl + C** and **Ctrl + V**. If you inadvertently give a keyboard command, rather than typing in, say, a capital 'V', you can click on the **Undo** button, on the Quick Access Toolbar, to correct the mistake.

Key word

Cut and *paste* **get their names from the publishing procedures used many years ago. Long strips of text called 'galleys' were actually cut up and then pasted on to blank page layouts.**

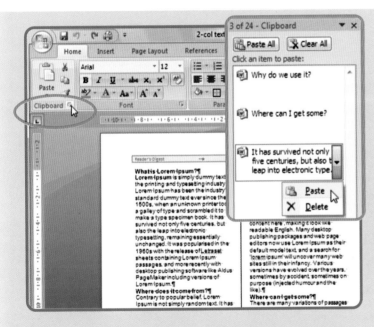

3 The Clipboard stores up to 24 items at any time, depending on their size. With the insertion point at the correct position in the text, click on the Clipboard dialogue box launcher. The Clipboard task pane appears and displays your cut and copied items as thumbnails. Click on the arrow next to the item you wish to 'Paste' then click on **Paste**. To remove the item click on **Delete**.

4 You can also use the 'Copy' and 'Paste' commands to move any text or images you want between two open Word documents. You can use the 'Paste Special' command in the 'Clipboard' group to paste text or images from the Clipboard to other programs or to a Web page, in the appropriate format.

AutoCorrect your text

Word's AutoCorrect feature detects and corrects common spelling mistakes, grammatical errors and incorrect use of capital letters. Furthermore, if you know that you often make specific typographical errors, such as typing 'seperate' instead of 'separate', you can add them to a list – AutoCorrect will then rectify the mistakes for you automatically as you type.

SEE ALSO...

● Find and replace p82

MAXIMUM EFFICIENCY
To make the most of the AutoCorrect feature, you should set it up to suit your own work requirements.

Go to the **Microsoft Office** button, select **Proofing** in the left pane and then click on **AutoCorrect Options**. Select the **AutoCorrect**

tab. The first four boxes relate to ways in which AutoCorrect can help with capitalisation. The most useful options are 'Capitalize first letter of sentences' and 'Capitalize names of days'. Click on a box to select an option.

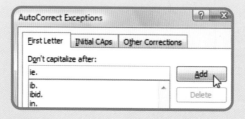

It is a good idea to set up exceptions to the rule. To do this, click on the **Exceptions** button and select the **First Letter** tab. There is a list of abbreviations in the 'Don't capitalize after' panel. To add to it, click in the top panel and type in any word commonly followed by a full stop – for example, the abbreviation 'ie'. Click on **Add**. To get rid of an item, select it and click on **Delete**.

The INitial CAps tab allows you to make exceptions to the autocorrection of two capital letters at the beginning of a word. The Other Corrections tab is for any words that AutoCorrect might detect as misspelt, but which you do not

wish to be changed. Click on **OK** to return to the AutoCorrect dialogue box.

Correcting common misspellings
In the AutoCorrect dialogue box under the AutoCorrect tab, click in the box next to 'Replace text as you type' if it isn't already selected, then look at the list of possible substitutions in the panel below.

The first few entries are keyboard formulas that you can enter to get certain symbols – for

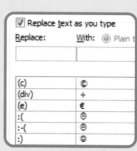

instance, if you type (c), Word will replace it with ©. Scroll down the list to see a number of common misspellings and typing errors that will be corrected

Watch out
When you enter words you commonly mistype in the 'Replace' panel, remember to make sure that they are not actual words – that is, those you might find in the dictionary. If they are, you may find some of your text has been corrected in error after you run AutoCorrect.

for you automatically if you use this option. You can even edit words in this list.

Select a word, click in the 'Replace' or 'With' panels, and type in your amendment. Then click on the **Replace** button. You can also **Delete** any spellings that are irrelevant to your work.

To add your own words, type your misspelling in the empty 'Replace' panel, and then type the

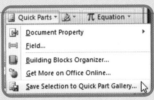

correction in the empty 'With' panel. Click on **Add** to add it to the list.

If you select 'Automatically use suggestions from the spelling checker', AutoCorrect will use corrections offered by the dictionary. Be aware that you might not always agree with the dictionary's substitutions, so it is a good idea to check any changes made as you type.

BUILDING BLOCKS
Use Building Blocks to store content from one document that you want to use regularly in other documents.

To create your own reusable Building Block, highlight the content that you want to store. If you want to capture the paragraph formatting (indents, alignment, line spacing, for example) as well, include the paragraph mark (¶) in your selection. Click on the **Insert** tab, select **Quick Parts** from the 'Text' group, then click on **Save Selection to Quick Part Gallery**. In the

Create New Building Block dialogue box, enter a name, select a gallery to use, choose a category, and in the 'Save in' options select a template to store the block. If you select 'Normal', the block will be available to all documents using that template. In 'Options', make a selection from the 'Insert' options, and click on **OK**.

Using your Building Blocks
Once you have created a block it's easy to use. In your open document, position the cursor where you want to insert a block. Click on the **Insert** tab, then on **Quick Parts** in the 'Text' group. Select your Building Block from the gallery, and it will appear at the cursor position.

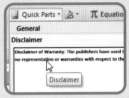

Editing an existing Building Block
If you have used a Building Block in your document, you can edit it and resave it to the gallery. Make your changes and highlight the text, click on **Quick Parts** and then on **Save Selection to Quick Part Gallery**. If you opt to use the same block name and gallery as before, the new version will overwrite the previous one.

Downloading Building Blocks
Assuming you have an active Internet connection, open or create a document. Click on the **Insert** tab, select **Quick Parts** from the 'Text' group, then click on **Get More on Office Online**. Your browser will display pages from

Microsoft Office Online with a range of available Building Blocks. Select a block, click on **Download** and follow the prompts. Repeat to download more blocks. When finished restart Word.

Bright idea
If you often use other styles of typed letters, such as superscript for fractions and dates, typing them into the 'AutoCorrect' box saves you having to select your text and change style manually.

Find and replace

When editing your work, you may realise that you have consistently misspelt a name or used the wrong sort of formatting. Or you may import a document from another program and find that it is full of unwanted formatting and characters. Word's 'Find and Replace' feature allows you to correct these errors with just a few keystrokes.

Close up
To run just a simple search, you can click on the Find tab instead. Or, select the Go To tab to find a specific location in your document, such as a page, line or comment.

BEFORE YOU START
Go to the **Home** tab and click on **Find** in the 'Editing' group to open the Find and Replace dialogue box. Select the **Replace** tab for more flexible search and text editing options.

1 Type your search word in the 'Find what' panel. Type a replacement word in the 'Replace with' panel. Click on **Replace**. The search word will be highlighted in your document. Click on **Find Next** to leave text unaltered, **Replace** to change it to the replacement word, or **Replace All** to replace all instances of the search word.

2 Click on **More** for further options – for instance, 'Match case' makes the search sensitive to capitals; 'Sounds like' will search for words that sound the same but are spelt differently.
The 'Special' button enables you to find and replace items such as paragraph and tab marks, fields and page breaks.

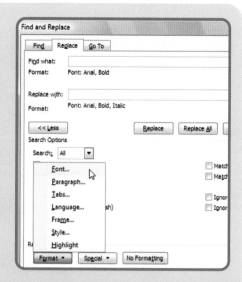

3 To search for formatted text, type your text in the 'Find what' panel, click on **Format** and select from the options. To replace formatting, type your text in the 'Replace with' panel and go to **Format** again. To search for and replace formatting alone, click in each of the panels before selecting a 'Format' option, but do not enter text.

Add a background

Giving your document a coloured or textured background is a great way to liven it up. You can write over the top and insert picture and text boxes. Although you cannot print Word's 'Backgrounds', the 'Watermark' function allows you to print a faded version, which is ideal for creating stylish personalised stationery.

SEE ALSO...
● *Add a picture* p84

BACKGROUNDS

Use the 'Background' feature to create coloured and textured pages for files that you don't need to print out.

With your document open, go to the **Page Layout** tab and click on **Page Color** in the 'Page Background' group. To add a solid colour to your document, just select one from the colours displayed. If you don't see the shade you want, click **More Colors**. For two tones, patterns and pictures, click on **Fill Effects**. Select the **Gradient**

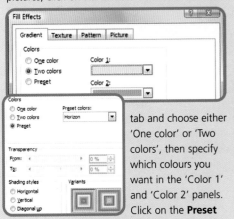

tab and choose either 'One color' or 'Two colors', then specify which colours you want in the 'Color 1' and 'Color 2' panels. Click on the **Preset** option to view different themes such as 'Desert' or 'Rainbow'. 'Shading styles' changes the way the two colours are mixed. View 'Variants' on the right and double-click to select a background.

For other options, click on the **Texture** tab and choose a pre-set background or click on the **Pattern** tab and select a colour from the 'Foreground' and 'Background' panels, then double-click on a pattern box to select it.

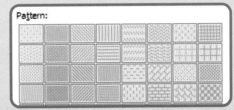

If you want to insert an image file as your page background, click on the **Picture** tab, then **Select Picture**. A dialogue box will open which lists all the images stored in your Pictures folder. Select a picture, click on **Insert** and then **OK**. Go to the **Page Layout** tab and click on **Watermark** in the 'Page Background' group.

WATERMARKS

Word's 'Watermark' feature places a faded version of your chosen graphic on the page, which can be printed.

Click on **Custom Watermark** in the drop-down list. In the Printed Watermark dialogue box you can select either a picture or text watermark. To insert a picture, click on **Picture watermark**,

then on **Select Picture**. Images stored in your Pictures folder are listed. Select a picture and click on **Insert**. Select a scale to size the watermark or leave at 'Auto' to fit the image to the margins. If your watermark is very pale, tick the 'washout' box, then click on **OK**. Any text that you type will appear in front of the watermark.

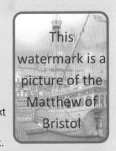

If you want to use text for your watermark, select from the pre-set options or click on **Custom watermark**. Click on **Text watermark**, key your text into the 'Text' panel, then select a font, size, colour and orientation (diagonal or horizontal), and then click on **OK**.

Add a picture

Inserting graphics or pictures into a document can instantly add impact and clarity to your subject. You can either use your own pictures, or choose from the vast gallery of ClipArt provided by Word. Desktop publishing is also made easy by allowing you to integrate illustrations and charts with your text, to produce professional-looking results.

SEE ALSO...
● *Add a background* p83

BEFORE YOU START
Open a document. You may already have a picture that you want to insert but don't worry if you haven't – you can easily find graphics stored on your computer, on a CD or on the Internet.

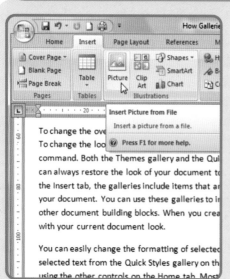

1 To add a graphic to your document, first position the cursor where you would like to insert the image. Next, go to the **Insert** tab and select **Picture** from the 'Illustrations' group. Use this to insert an image stored on your PC, a CD-ROM or other removeable storage device.

2 The Insert Picture dialogue box appears on screen. It automatically shows your Pictures folder, where you will see some sample images. Click on the drop-down list in the 'Look in' panel to browse for your image file.

Click on **Views** on the Menu bar to select the best viewing options for your pictures. Click on a picture to select it, then on **Insert**.

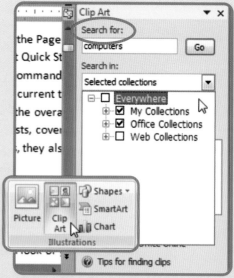

3 Alternatively, to insert a picture from Word's Clip Gallery, go to the **Insert** tab and choose **Clip Art** from the 'Illustrations' group. The Clip Art Task Pane appears. Type a keyword into the 'Search for' panel. Then select where you want to search in the 'Search in' panel.

Text-Wrapping

You can wrap the text around the graphic in different ways. Click on **Text Wrapping** in the 'Arrange' group, scroll down the list and click on a style to select it.

Watch out

Although it is fine to use ClipArt in documents such as newsletters and flyers, it is not legal to use it for promotional or marketing material, nor can you publish a document containing it.

4 Now click on the **Go** button next to your keyword. Your results will be displayed as thumbnails in the panel below. Hover your mouse over a thumbnail for information on that image. Select your choice of picture and then click on **Insert**.

5 If you have an Internet connection click on **Clip art on Office Online** for a greater selection of images. In the Microsoft Office Online website, type your keyword into the search bar and click on **Search**. Add a tick to select images, then click on **Download**, and follow the prompts.

6 To resize an image, click on it, then click and drag on a handle (above). Use the controls in the 'Adjust' group to adjust brightness, contrast and colours. Right-click on the image and choose **Edit Picture**. You can now select individual elements and edit them. Experiment to achieve different effects.

Print your work

You are now ready to print out your pages. For the best results, take time to consider the appropriate layout for your document and to view how it will look before printing. Most printers allow you to vary the size of paper you use and to print envelopes and sticky labels. Depending on your printer, you may even be able to produce high quality photographic prints.

SEE ALSO...
- *Save your work* p60
- *Format a document* p68

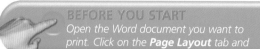

BEFORE YOU START
Open the Word document you want to print. Click on the **Page Layout** tab and in the 'Page Setup' group click on **Margins**, then **Custom Margins**. 'Preview' shows how the page will look.

1 The margins are set to default values. To select a new value, click the up or down arrows beside each panel, or highlight the existing value and type a new number. Under 'Orientation', select **Portrait** (vertical) or **Landscape** (horizontal). See the difference between these two options in the 'Preview' section (below).

2 Select the **Paper** tab, and check that the paper size is set to 'A4'. If it isn't, or you want a different paper size, click the down arrow and select the correct paper size.

If you want to print the first page of your document on pre-printed paper (like a letterhead), you can choose the correct printer tray for that particular paper in the 'Paper source' panel.

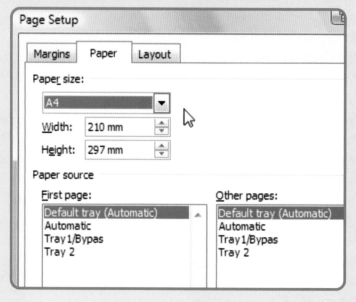

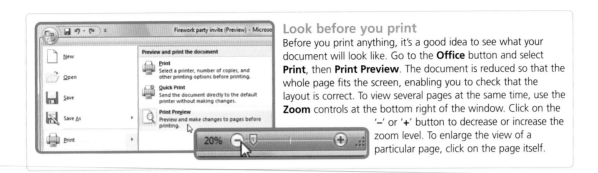

Look before you print

Before you print anything, it's a good idea to see what your document will look like. Go to the **Office** button and select **Print**, then **Print Preview**. The document is reduced so that the whole page fits the screen, enabling you to check that the layout is correct. To view several pages at the same time, use the **Zoom** controls at the bottom right of the window. Click on the '–' or '+' button to decrease or increase the zoom level. To enlarge the view of a particular page, click on the page itself.

---

4 Go to the **Office** button and click on **Print**. Select your printer in the 'Name' panel. Under 'Page range', you can choose to print the whole document ('All'), the page you are on ('Current page'), or a range of pages ('Pages'). To print a range, you will need to enter the page numbers. You can print an area of text that you have highlighted by using the 'Selection' button.

3 Finally, click the **Layout** tab to change the position of the headers and footers in the 'From edge' section. Under 'Page' in the 'Vertical alignment' box, you can choose how your text is positioned between the top and bottom page margins. Text is automatically aligned to the top. You can number your lines and create borders for sections of text or whole pages. Click on **OK** to finish.

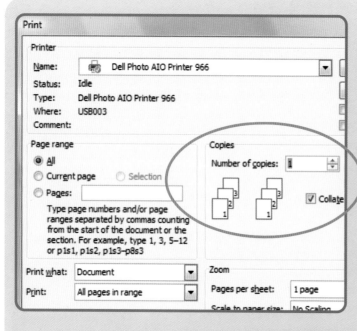

5 To print more than one copy of a document, click on the up arrow in the 'Number of copies' panel, or highlight the figure and type in the number of copies you want. Select the **Collate** option if you want your copies printed in page order within each set.

6 For double-sided printing, scroll down the options in the 'Print' box and select **Odd pages**. Pages 1, 3, 5 and so on will then print. Once these are done, turn the printed sheets over, place them in your printer again and select **Even pages** in the Print dialogue box. Click on **OK** to print pages 2, 4, 6 and so on.

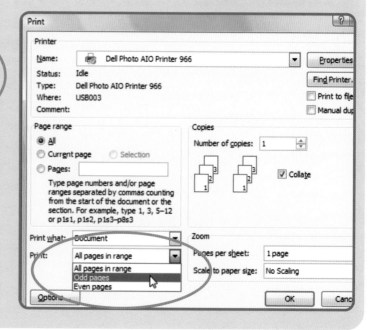

Excel

Explore the program

Although Excel 2007 is designed to be intuitive, you will be able to use it more confidently and efficiently if you first take time to find your way around the elements of the main document window, such as the toolbar of commands called the 'Ribbon'. This will give you a better understanding of the many powerful features Excel has to offer.

SEE ALSO...
● *What is Excel? p16*

BEFORE YOU START
You may have a shortcut for Excel on your Desktop. Look out for an 'Excel' icon, with a small arrow in the bottom left-hand corner. Double-click on this to run Excel.

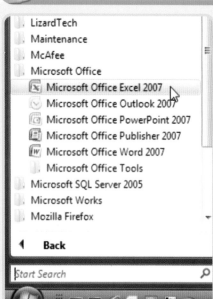

2 While the program data is being loaded into the memory from the hard disk, you will see a splash screen. This is a small window that tells you which version of Excel you are using. After a few seconds this window disappears and the program continues to load.

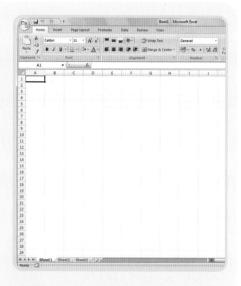

3 When Excel has loaded, a new blank document opens. At the top is the Ribbon, with groups of associated commands under each tab. To the right and at the bottom of the grid are the scroll bars. Directly above and to the left of the grid are the column letters and row numbers, which give each cell a unique reference.

1 To launch Excel, click on the **Start** button at the bottom left of your screen, then on **All Programs**. Move the mouse pointer up to highlight **Microsoft Office** and click once. Then click on **Microsoft Office Excel 2007**.

GETTING AROUND IN EXCEL

If you are not familiar with spreadsheets, it's a good idea to acquaint yourself with the basic features before you get started.

Using the mouse

The mouse is the primary tool for clicking on, moving and selecting items in Excel. It should be used on a mouse mat and orientated with its 'tail' pointing towards the screen. When following the instructions in this book, 'click' means to single-click on the left mouse button; 'right-click' indicates that you should use the right mouse button.

The pointer in Excel is an outlined cross (see left, top). This allows you to select a cell or range of cells. When you are entering or editing text, the pointer changes to a tall capital I (see left, centre). Clicking with this pointer positions the insertion point, a flashing vertical bar, ready for new text to be entered. When you move the mouse pointer over the buttons on the Ribbon, it turns into the familiar Windows arrow (see left, bottom). Use this to click on items.

Selecting cells

Excel always opens with the top left cell selected in a new blank spreadsheet. This cell is called A1 because the cell is at the intersection of column A and row 1. All the cells on a spreadsheet have a unique reference, which is derived from their column letter and row number. You can see the reference for the currently selected cell in the 'Name Box', to the left of the Formula Bar.

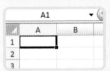

The currently selected cell has a dark black outline. To enter text in it, just start typing. To move to (or 'select') another cell, position the cross-shaped mouse pointer over it, click once and start typing. It is also possible to move to another cell by using the keyboard arrow keys.

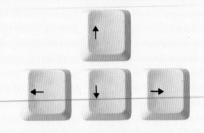

To select a range of cells – A3 to F20 for example – click on A3 and hold down the left mouse button. Then drag the mouse to the right and down to cell F20. The cells will be highlighted. If the range is larger than the window, select the top left cell in the range, hold down the **Shift** key on your keyboard, then move down the spreadsheet using the scroll bars until the bottom right cell in the range is visible and click once on that cell.

Moving around a spreadsheet

A spreadsheet is a vast grid of cells stretching across and down the screen – there are 1,048,576 rows and 16,384 columns, making over 171 million cells – so it is easy to get lost. Pressing the **Ctrl** and **Home** keys together takes you back to cell A1. You can use the horizontal and vertical scroll bars to move around the page by clicking on the arrows at either end of the scroll bars, by dragging the box up and down, or by clicking on the small bar above or below the box to move up or down a screen at a time.

Excel's commands

The main way to give Excel instructions is by using the buttons on the Ribbon. These buttons are organised within tabs and grouped together by similar function. They allow you to carry out all the tasks you require in Excel, from creating spreadsheets to editing, styling and structuring your work. Click once on a tab to view 'groups' of buttons for related tasks.

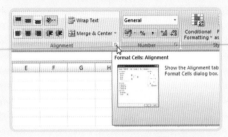

Some of the groups have a small arrow at the bottom right-hand corner – this is called a dialogue box launcher. When you click on it a dialogue box appears containing additional commands related to that group.

If you are unsure what a button on the Ribbon does, hover the mouse

pointer over it and a helpful ToolTip will pop up giving a description of the button's function and a keyboard shortcut, for example, **Ctrl+C**. A keyboard shortcut is a quick way of performing a command. To use a shortcut, hold down the **Ctrl** key at the bottom left of your keyboard and press the relevant letter – in this case, **C**.

COMMAND TABS

All the tasks you could want to perform in Excel can be carried out by clicking on buttons on the Ribbon. These buttons are organised into groups and are found under the different tabs.

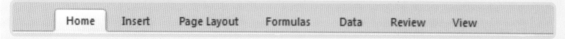

Before you start using Excel, it's a good idea to click on each tab on the Ribbon to familiarise yourself with the options it displays. Most commands have icons illustrating their function.

The Home tab

This gives you access to basic editing and formatting functions, such as copying and pasting data, formatting cells and changing fonts.

The Insert tab

The options on this tab allow you to insert items such as tables, illustrations and charts in your spreadsheet.

The Page Layout tab

This tab contains options for laying out your pages, changing the scale of a document so it will print on one page and applying pre-formatted 'themes' to style your work.

The Formulas tab

Here you can access a wide range of functions and formulas to enhance your spreadsheets.

The Quick Access Toolbar

This toolbar appears in the top left corner of every window in Excel 2007 and contains, by default, three commands ('Save', 'Undo' and 'Redo'), plus a button which allows you to customise the toolbar.

To add a command, click the **Customize Quick Access Toolbar** button and choose a command from the list, or click on **More Commands**. In the Excel Options dialogue box that appears, choose a category from the list in the left pane, then select a command. Click on **Add** and then on **OK**.

The Data tab

This tab allows you to perform complex tasks, such as sorting or filtering data. It also allows you to import data from other programs.

The Review tab

This lets you check the spelling and grammar in your documents, as well as adding comments to spreadsheets and tracking changes made by others.

The View tab

Here you can choose how documents are displayed and whether elements such as the ruler and gridlines are shown or hidden.

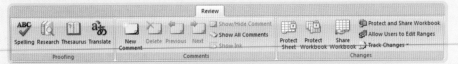

CONTEXTUAL TABS

The tabs displayed on the Ribbon change depending on the action you are performing, and new tabs may appear providing additional commands related to that action. For example, when you are editing a table the Table Tools contextual tab is displayed and if an image is selected in a document, the Picture Tools contextual tab appears.

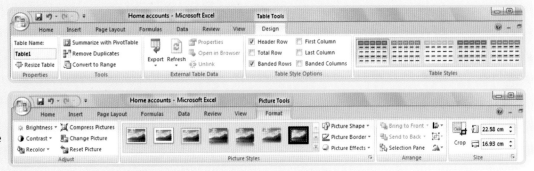

The Mini Toolbar

Whenever you have text selected the Mini Toolbar will appear close by. It gives immediate access to the most commonly used text formatting options.

Highlight some text and, with the mouse pointer positioned over the highlighted area, slowly move the mouse upwards. The Mini Toolbar will gradually appear over the highlighted area. Click on one of the options to style your text.

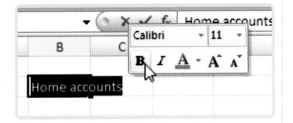

Entering data

Getting your information into Excel is simple – just click on a cell anywhere on your spreadsheet and start typing. Then select another cell or press the Return key to confirm the data. If you need to edit your data, either make the changes in the cell, or type them in the Formula Bar. You can move around using the keyboard arrow keys or by clicking with the mouse.

SEE ALSO...
- *What is Excel?* *p16*
- *Explore the program* *p90*
- *Excel formulas* *p98*

BEFORE YOU START
Have all the information that you might want to enter into your spreadsheet to hand. Don't worry about organising it, as Excel can do that for you afterwards.

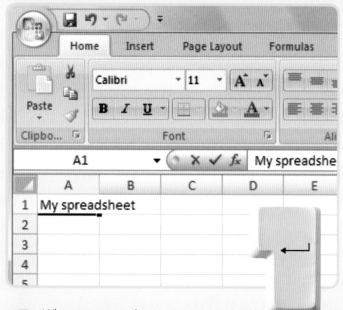

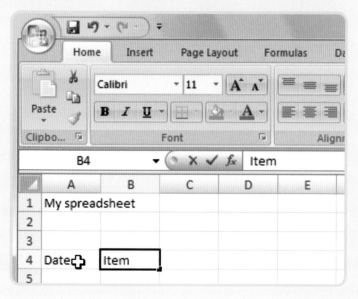

1 When you open the Excel program, cell A1 is always selected in the top-left corner of a blank spreadsheet. You can type the title of your spreadsheet straight into this cell, or select another one by clicking on it. When you've finished typing, press **Return** or click on another cell. You can also select cells by using the keyboard arrow keys.

2 As a rule, keep row 1 empty except for your title and start entering your data a few rows down. Press the **Down** arrow key on your keyboard a few times to move down, or click on a cell with your mouse, and start typing. Use the **Right** arrow or the **Tab** key on your computer keyboard to move across the row to enter your column headings.

Undoing mistakes

If you start typing in a cell that already contains some data, you will replace that data with whatever you type. If you accidentally delete the contents of a cell, press the **Esc** key or click the **Cancel** button on the Formula Bar to restore them. If you have moved away from the cell or pressed **Return**, use the **Undo** button to reverse your actions one step at a time.

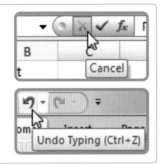

Cancel

Undo Typing (Ctrl+Z)

Close up
If you are entering a lot of data arranged in rows, use the Tab key to move to the right. When you press Return at the end of a row, Excel will automatically move you to the beginning of the next row down.

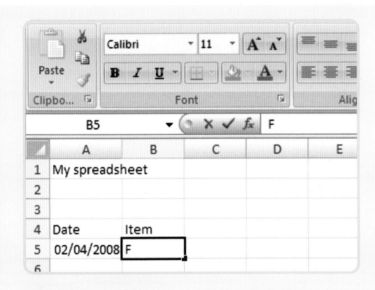

4 To edit the contents of a cell, you can either double-click on the cell, or select it and click on its text in the Formula Bar (below). If you can't edit a cell by double-clicking on it, go to the **Office** button and choose **Excel Options**. Then click on **Advanced**, put a tick next to 'Allow editing directly in cells' and click on **OK**. Position the insertion point (the flashing vertical bar) by clicking with the mouse, and use the **Backspace** key (above) to delete text before the insertion point and the **Delete** key to delete text after the insertion point. If you want to replace the entire contents of a cell, just select it and start typing.

3 Use the **Shift** key to type a capital letter and to select the symbols on the upper portion of the punctuation and number keys. Don't use the mathematical operator symbols – plus **(+)**, minus **(-)**, multiply **(*)**, divide **(/)** and equals **(=)** – unless you are entering a formula (see page 96) or a date. Otherwise Excel will display the '#NAME?' error message.

Save your work

When you save a spreadsheet, its digital data is copied from the computer's memory to the hard disk drive, where it is stored until you next open the file. If you don't save your work, all the data will be lost when you exit the program or switch off your PC. Remember to save regularly so you don't lose important work if your computer crashes.

SEE ALSO...

● *Entering data* p94

BEFORE YOU START
To save your spreadsheet, click on the **Office** button and choose **Save**. You can also click on *'Save'* on the Quick Access Toolbar, or press *Ctrl* and *S* on the keyboard.

1 The first time you save a file, the Save As dialogue box appears. Type a recognisable file name for your spreadsheet in the 'File name' box – you can use up to 256 characters including spaces, but you can't use symbols such as **?** and *****. Excel chooses your Documents folder as the default location for your file, and this is automatically selected in the bar at the top of the window.

2 Your Documents folder is a good place to store spreadsheets, but it can become cluttered, making files difficult to locate. Choose a different location by selecting another folder from the 'Folders' list on the left of the window. Alternatively, create a new folder. Click on the **New Folder** button, type an appropriate name for your folder and click on the **Save** button. Excel creates your folder and changes the folder in the 'Save in' box to your new folder name.

Watch out
Once you have saved your spreadsheet, if you want to save any subsequent changes to the document, click on the **Office** button and choose **Save**. However, if you have edited the spreadsheet and want to save it as a different version of the current document, choose **Save As** from the Office menu to make a new file. Otherwise you will save over your previous work.

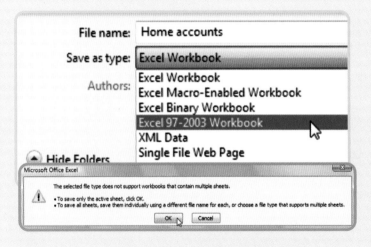

3 Under 'File name' is the 'Save as type' box, which has a drop-down list of different formats for saving your file. You should leave 'Excel Workbook' selected unless you are saving a file for someone with an older version of Excel, or someone who doesn't have a spreadsheet program, in which case you might choose to save the file as a 'PDF'. If you choose a different file type, you may see a message appear, warning that the selected file type does not support workbooks that contain multiple sheets. Click on **OK** if you want to go ahead with the save or click on **Cancel** and choose another format.

4 When you are happy with your file name, folder and file type, click on the **Save** button. The Save As dialogue box closes and the file name is displayed in the Title bar at the top of the window. To save your work, you can press **Ctrl + S** or click on the **Save** button on the Quick Access Toolbar.

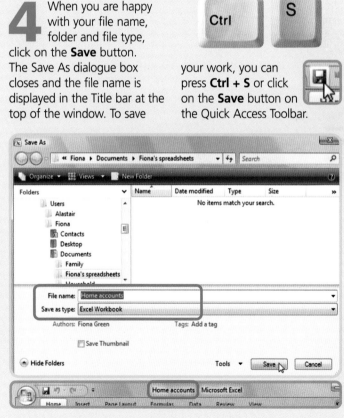

Excel formulas

Each cell in an Excel spreadsheet has its own address, made up of its column and row references. This means that a calculation in one cell can refer to other cells – for instance, A1 could display the result of A2 + A3. In fact, using just the simple mathematical operators – plus, minus, multiply and divide – you can build an extremely useful spreadsheet.

SEE ALSO...
- *Using AutoSum p100*
- *Cut, copy and paste p102*

BEFORE YOU START
Create a new spreadsheet and carefully copy the column headings illustrated in Step 1 below. Enter some of your monthly shopping items, prices and amounts.

1 Once you have entered some data into your spreadsheet you can perform some calculations on the values in the cells. Click in cell E4 under 'Total' and type '='. This tells Excel you are about to enter a formula. Then click on C4 under 'Price', type '*' (**Shift + 8** on the keyboard), click on D4 under 'Amount' and press **Return**.

2 The formula '=C4*D4' in cell E4 tells Excel to multiply the contents of C4 by the contents of D4 and display the result in E4, which in this case is 7. Excel will recalculate this value every time you change a value in C4 or D4. Try changing the value in cell C4 to '2' and the value in cell D4 to '5' – the total in E4 will change automatically each time you enter a new number.

3 Change the price and amount back to the original values and move to cell E5. Instead of clicking to select the cells to be used in the calculation you can enter them directly, so type in '=C5*D5' and press **Return**. The result will then appear. Continue to add formulas until you get to the end of your list.

Copying formulas

A quick way of copying a formula to an adjacent cell is to use the Fill Handle: move the mouse pointer over the small black square in the bottom right corner of the selected cell and the pointer will change to a black **+** sign. Click and drag it to an adjacent cell where you want the formula to be pasted and release the mouse button.

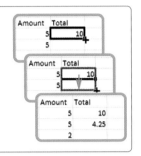

Watch out

When constructing formulas that involve multiplication and division as well as addition and subtraction, make sure you bear in mind the 'order of operations' – multiplication and division must be completed before addition and subtraction. If you want to create a formula that adds two numbers together before multiplying them by a third number, you must enclose the addition in brackets because Excel performs the calculation in brackets first. For example, '=(3+4)*2'.

4 Once all your item prices have been multiplied by the amount of each item, you need to create a monthly total. Click in the cell under the last item in your list in column B and type 'Monthly Total'. Then, move across to column E and type '='. Click on cell E4 and type '+'. Next, click on cell E5 and type another '+'. Continue to add all the items in your list and then press **Return**.

5 The total of your monthly spending appears in column E. This number will be recalculated every time you change a number in your data – try altering a few numbers to see how it works. Now add another formula to subtract your monthly total from your monthly budget. Click in the cell in column B under 'Monthly Total' and type 'Monthly Budget'. Enter the value of your monthly budget in the same row in column E – in this case, '50'.

Item	Price	Amount	Total
Toilet rolls	1.75	4	7
Bread	0.85	5	4.25
Butter	1.65	2	3.3
Eggs	0.86	4	3.44
Teabags	2.32	3	6.96
Monthly Total			24.95
Monthly Budget			

Item	Price	Amount	Total
Toilet rolls	1.75	4	7
Bread	0.85	5	4.25
Butter	1.65	2	3.3
Eggs	0.86	4	3.44
Teabags	2.32	3	6.96
Monthly Total			24.95
Monthly Budget			50

Item	Price	Amount	Total
Toilet rolls	1.75	4	7
Bread	0.85	5	4.25
Butter	1.65	2	3.3
Eggs	0.86	4	3.44
Teabags	2.32	3	6.96
Monthly Total			24.95
Monthly Budget			50
Monthly Surplus			=E10-E9

Item	Price	Amount	Total
Toilet rolls	1.75	4	7
Bread	0.85	5	4.25
Butter	1.65	2	3.3
Eggs	0.86	4	3.44
Teabags	2.32	3	6.96
Monthly Total			24.95
Monthly Budget			50
Monthly Surplus			25.05
			6.2375

6 Now click under 'Monthly Budget' and type 'Monthly Surplus'. Move to column E and type an '='. Then click on your monthly budget amount, type '-', click on the monthly total amount and press **Return**. Here, the formula '=E10-E9' tells Excel to subtract the value in E9 from the value in E10. Type '=E9/4' under your surplus to divide your monthly expenditure by 4. This calculates your weekly expenditure.

Using AutoSum

Performing simple addition with Excel is easy using the formula demonstrated on the previous pages. However, if you want to add up a long list of values it can be time-consuming to enter all the cell references and plus signs into a formula. Fortunately, Excel includes an AutoSum function that instantly totals a column or row of values.

SEE ALSO...
- *Excel formulas* *p98*
- *Cut, copy and paste* *p102*

BEFORE YOU START
The example below uses Excel's AutoSum function to check your bank statement and work out your expenditure. Start by opening a new spreadsheet.

1 Type a title, such as 'Bank Statement', for your spreadsheet in cell A1 and add the column headings 'Item', 'In', and 'Out'. Then copy the data from the example above. Once you have finished, select cell C2 and then click on the **AutoSum** button in the 'Editing' group on the Ribbon.

2 When you click on the **AutoSum** button, Excel inserts a SUM **function** in the selected cell. Between the brackets, Excel expects to see some information telling it which cells contain the values you want to be added together. Click in cell C4, then, keeping the mouse button pressed down, drag the mouse pointer down to cell C8, release the button and press **Return**.

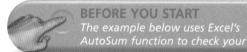

3 Excel now adds up the values in your 'In' column and displays the result in cell C2. If you select cell C2 and look in the Formula Bar, you will see that C2 actually contains the AutoSum function '=SUM(C4:C8)'. We have placed the totals above the data so you can add more entries to the bottom of the list easily without having to insert extra rows.

Key word
*Formulas **are equations,
such as '=A1+A2', that
perform calculations on***
*values in the spreadsheet. Functions **are
pre-defined formulas built in to Excel, for
example, '=SUM(A1:A3)'.***

Watch out
When extending a range, be careful
to click on the bottom corner of the
blue box and not the edge, otherwise
you will move the whole of the blue
box down. If you accidentally move the
box, click on the **Undo** button to reverse your action.

5 Next, move to cell E2 and type
an '='. Click on cell C2, type a '-'
and then click on cell D2. Then
press **Return**. Excel will now subtract
your 'Out' total from your 'In' total. The
formula should read '=C2-D2'. As you
add more items to your list of entries,
Excel recalculates all the formulas and
functions for you.

4 Now use the Fill Handle (see
Copying **formulas**, page 99) to
copy the AutoSum function into
cell D2: click and drag the square at the
bottom right corner of cell C2 across to
D2. Excel copies the function and adds
up your outgoings. The total will be
displayed in cell D2 and, if you look in
the Formula Bar, you will see the
function '=SUM(D4:D8)'.

6 If you want to add some data
beyond row 8 in your
spreadsheet, it will not be
included in the SUM function because
we limited its range in step 1. To edit the
formula, double-click on cell C2. A blue
border appears around cells C4 to C8. By
clicking and dragging either of the little
squares at the bottom corners, it is
possible to extend the formula's range,
ready for any new data. Copy the new
formula across to cell D2 (see step 4).

Cut, copy and paste

Using Excel's Cut, Copy and Paste tools and the Office Clipboard, you can quickly move blocks of figures or text around your spreadsheet. You can also copy a formula and paste it into several cells in one go while Excel automatically changes its references. This saves time and effort if you need to move data or enter identical formulas in multiple cells.

SEE ALSO...
- *Explore the program* p90
- *Excel formulas* p98
- *Columns and rows* p106
- *Insert a comment* p120

BEFORE YOU START
Enter the months 'Jan', 'Feb' and 'Mar' in cells B3, C3 and D3. Then type in some sample figures under each column heading to use as test data.

1 Select cell B2 and insert an AutoSum function to total the range B4 to B6: click on the **AutoSum** button in the 'Editing' group, click and drag to select cells B4 to B6 and press **Return**. The result appears in cell B2. Then click

on the **Copy** button in the 'Clipboard' group. You will see a dotted line around cell B2. Select cells C2 to D2, click on the **Paste** button and Excel pastes your function across the row and adjusts it so it adds up the cells in the relevant columns.

2 To move data rather than copy it, use the 'Cut' command. When you cut data, it remains in its original location on the spreadsheet until you click on **Paste** – then the original data is deleted. Try moving all your data down one row in your spreadsheet: select the range

B2 to D6, click on **Cut** in the 'Clipboard' group. Then select cell B3 and click on **Paste**. The data is moved to its new location. Note that copied or cut data is pasted with reference to the cell that was selected when you clicked **Paste**, in this case, B3.

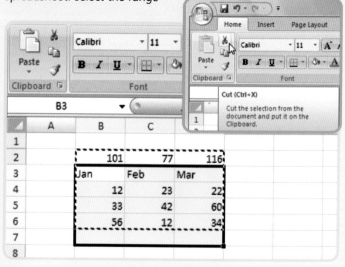

Contextual menu

Instead of using the 'Clipboard' group buttons, you can use the options on the contextual menu to cut, copy and paste. Right-click with the mouse and a drop-down menu of options appears related to the action previously carried out. Scroll down the menu and select an item. Alternatively, hold down the **Ctrl** key on the keyboard and press **X** for cut, **C** for copy and **V** for paste.

Expert advice

You may want to paste a formula without Excel changing the range of cells to which it refers. For example, you might want to refer always to cell A1 if it contains the current VAT rate. In your formula, insert the '$' symbol before both the letter and the number so, in this case, it becomes 'A1'. This 'fixes' the reference so that you can paste the formula anywhere and it will always refer to the specified cell for its calculations.

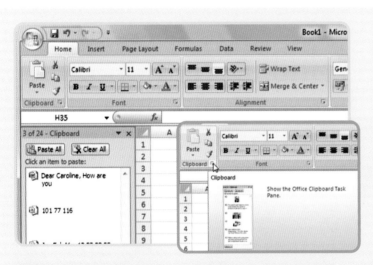

3 When you cut or copy anything in a Microsoft Office application it is placed on the Clipboard. You can place up to 24 items here. If you exceed 24, the oldest data will be lost. To see the Clipboard, click on the dialogue box launcher located at the bottom right of the 'Clipboard' group. It will appear in the Task Pane on the left of the window. Here you can review all the items you have copied and cut – including those from other Office programs – and paste them wherever you like. Select a cell in your spreadsheet and click on the item to be pasted from the Clipboard.

4 The advantage of copying and pasting in Excel is that all the formatting and formulas are copied as well as the cell contents. However, you can choose exactly how you want your data to be pasted using the 'Paste Special' feature. For example, you can choose to paste the formats only. Click on the arrow below 'Paste' and choose **Paste Special**, then use the radio buttons and tick boxes to select how you want your data to be pasted – 'Formulas' pastes the data without any formatting, 'Values' pastes the results of formulas only, 'Comments' pastes a cell comment (see page 120), and 'Transpose' turns a column into a row or vice versa (see page 107).

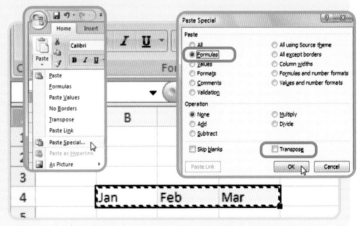

Columns and rows

Excel's grid-like structure of columns and rows makes it ideal for storing and presenting data. You can easily change the width of a column and the height of a row just by clicking and dragging. Excel also keeps track of your formulas and formatting so that inserting a row or a column doesn't change your calculations or cause problems with spreadsheet design.

SEE ALSO...
● *Format your data* p108
● *Aligning data* p112

BEFORE YOU START
Enter some sample text and numbers in several columns in your spreadsheet. You will need to make some text entries wider than the standard column width.

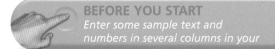

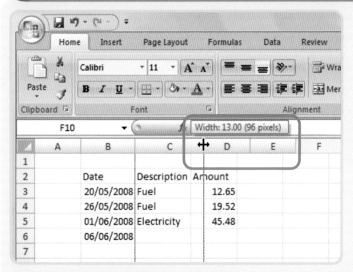

1 In our example above, we have entered the column headings in Excel's default font size (11pt). However, 'Description' is too long to fit in its column. To make column C wider, move the mouse pointer over the boundary between the C and D column headers until it turns into a double-headed arrow. Then click and drag the boundary to the right – a dotted line shows your new column boundary, and a pop-up box indicates the new width in standard characters and pixels.

2 To reduce the width of the 'Amount' column, click on the boundary between columns D and E and drag it to the left until the new column width looks right. If, after changing a column width, some numbers are represented as '####', click the boundary again and widen the column slightly until all the entries fit.

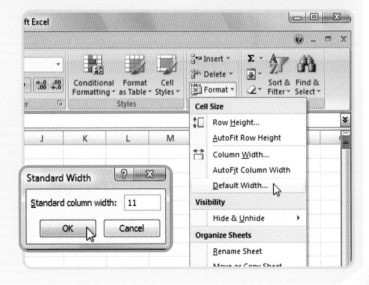

3 Excel automatically increases the height of rows if you increase the size of the font you are using (see page 110). However, you may want to increasethe height of a row yourself to add a little space, for example between the spreadsheet title and the column headings. Click on the boundary between the row headers, in this case rows 2 and 3, and then drag it downwards. This will increase the height of row 2 to create a little more space above the column headings. Again, a pop-up box displays the height as you drag.

4 To set all the columns in a new spreadsheet to a standard width, click on the arrow next to 'Format' in the 'Cells' group and choose **Default Width**. In the Standard Width dialogue box, Excel's default column width of 8.43 is displayed. Type in the value you require – in our example we have entered 11 – and click on **OK**. All columns will now be set to the selected width. Note that if you have previously adjusted the width of a column, it will not be affected by this action.

Close up
You can insert more than one column or row at a time. Click on a column or row header and drag to select the number of columns or rows you want to insert. Then in the 'Cells' group click on the arrow next to Insert and choose Insert Sheet Columns or Insert Sheet Rows.

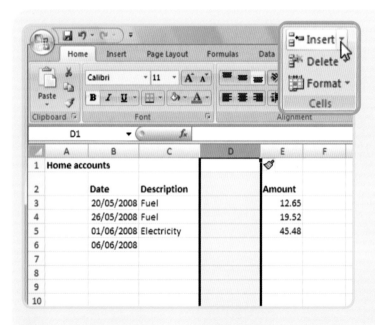

5 To insert an extra column in your spreadsheet, select the column to the right of where you want the new column by clicking on its header. For example, to insert a column between columns C and D, select column D. Then click on **Insert** in the 'Cells' group and the contents of D are moved to E and a new blank column is inserted after column C.

6 To insert a new row, select the row below where you want the new row, then click on **Insert** in the 'Cells' group. Excel moves your data down a row and inserts a new row. Don't worry about any formulas being moved, as the references are automatically changed to take into account the extra columns or rows. To remove a column or a row, select it by clicking on its header and then click on **Delete** in the 'Cells' group. Excel moves your data and adjusts the formulas for you.

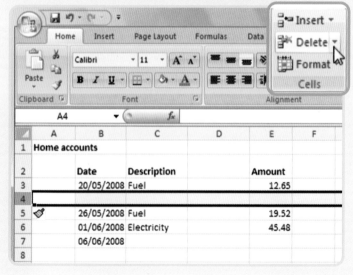

Bright idea
If you have inserted a new row and want to insert another one somewhere else, a quick way of doing this is to use the keyboard shortcut Ctrl + Y, which repeats your last action. Click on the row header below where you want the new row and use the keyboard shortcut to save time.

Watch out
If you insert several columns or rows at a time, bear in mind that Excel will only adjust the formulas if you insert rows or columns between others referred to in the formulas. For example, if an AutoSum function adds up the values in C2 to C5 it is best to insert a single row before C5, and use the **Ctrl + Y** keyboard shortcut to repeat the action.

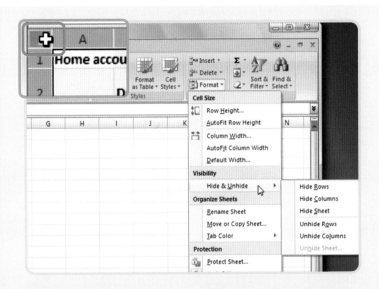

7 If you want to conceal a row but not delete it – for example, if it contains data you don't want to print or to be visible – click on the row header to select it. Click on **Format** in the 'Cells' group and select **Hide & Unhide** then **Hide Rows**. To make the hidden row visible again, select the whole sheet by clicking on the **Select All** button in the top left corner, and click on **Format**, select **Hide & Unhide** and then click on **Unhide Rows**. The same process can be applied to columns.

8 If you have typed some data in a row but then want it to be in a column, Excel has a handy transpose feature that swaps columns to rows and vice versa. Copy the data you want to transpose by selecting it and then clicking on **Cut** in the 'Clipboard' group. Next, select a cell on a blank area, click on the arrow below **Paste** and choose **Paste Special**. Put a tick next to 'Transpose' and click on **OK**.

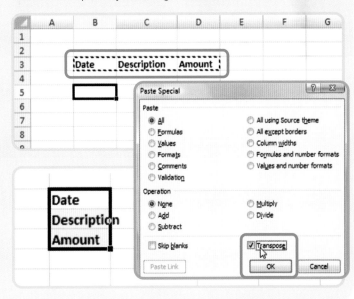

Format your data

Excel needs to know the type of data stored in each of its cells in order to display, sort and calculate it correctly. When you enter certain information – such as dates – Excel will often apply the correct formatting automatically. However, there is a surefire way to make certain Excel formats all your categories of data correctly, no matter how you type them in.

SEE ALSO...
● *Columns and rows* p104
● *Style your data* p110
● *Aligning data* p112

BEFORE YOU START
Type the headings 'Date', 'Description' and 'Amount' in cells B2 to D2. This example shows you how to format cells to display data as dates and currency.

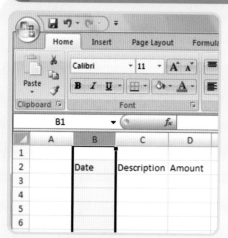

1 Once you have typed the headings for the columns of data in your spreadsheet, it's a good idea to format the cells before you start entering the data. That way, Excel will automatically insert the '£' sign in the prices, and will also differentiate between text and dates. Highlight the column of cells which will contain your dates by clicking on the column header – in this case B.

2 Click on the **Format** button in the 'Cells' group and then on **Format Cells**. When the Format Cells dialogue box opens, click on the **Number** tab and choose **Date** from the 'Category' list on the left. You will see a selection of date formats appear in the 'Type' list on the right. Scroll down until you see a format you like and click on it. Use a short version (shown below) for large spreadsheets.

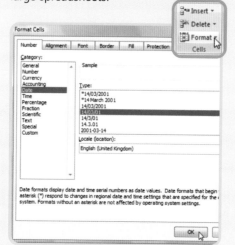

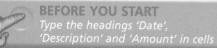

3 Click on the **OK** button to apply the formatting to the selected cells. Now try entering the date in cell B3 as '20 Jan 2008'. Excel recognises you have typed in a date and formats it as '20/01/08', the format we selected in step 2. Any date typed in column B will be formatted this way.

Watch out
If your date column appears to be full of strange numbers, you may have formatted it incorrectly. Don't change any data, just select the date column, click on the **Format** button in the 'Cells' group and choose **Format Cells**. Then click on the **Number** tab and make sure that 'Date' is selected in the list on the left.

Expert advice
Try out the other formatting options under the Number tab in the Format Cells dialogue box. You can instruct Excel to round numbers to two decimal points, format your numbers as times with AM and PM, or even display figures as fractions or percentages.

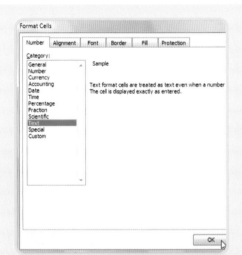

5 Select the 'Amount' column by clicking on the D column header, then open the Format Cells dialogue box again and, under the Number tab, choose **Currency** from the 'Category' list. Select a **£** sign from the list next to 'Symbol' and then choose how you would like negative numbers to be displayed – select the first option. Click on **OK**.

4 Click on 'C' at the top of the 'Description' column to select the whole column. Then click on the **Format** button, then **Format Cells** and, with the Number tab selected, click on **Text** in the 'Category' list on the left and then on **OK**. This ensures that everything entered in the 'Description' column, even if it looks like a number, will be treated and sorted as text.

6 Now start entering data into your spreadsheet – type dates in the first column, text entries in the second and amounts in the third. You will see that Excel automatically formats each new entry according to the pre-selected cell formatting. Note that text is aligned to the left of each cell and numbers to the right. It is easy to change the alignment settings – see page 112 for details.

Style your data

No matter how well your spreadsheet calculates its data, the results are wasted if its contents are not clearly presented and legible. Excel includes a wide range of data formatting tools, including options for sizing, styling and colouring data, which enable you to turn a bewildering array of figures and calculations into an easy-to-follow and logical worksheet.

SEE ALSO...
- *Format your data p108*
- *Colours and patterns p114*

BEFORE YOU START
Enter some sample data into your spreadsheet and select the cells by clicking and dragging the mouse from the first cell to the last cell in your desired range.

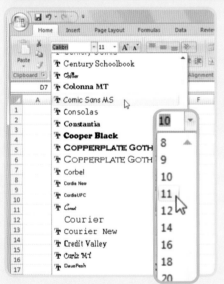

1 To change font type and size, click on the **Font** and **Font Size** boxes in the 'Font' group. Click the small downward arrow to the right of each box to choose from a list of options. If you want to format some data within a specific cell, highlight only the words or figures you want to format.

2 Click on the **Bold**, **Italic** and **Underline** font style buttons to quickly style selected data. However, bear in mind that both italic and underline can be difficult to read on a large page of relatively small data.

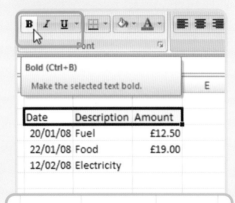

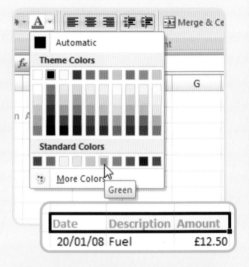

3 You can colour selected data by clicking the down arrow beside the **A** button on the far right of the bottom row of the 'Font' group and choosing a colour from the pop-up palette. Note that if you click the **A** button instead of the arrow, your data will change to the colour of the bar underneath the **A**, which indicates the last colour selected.

Choosing a font

Excel uses the Calibri font by default. This means that all data will be Calibri and is sized at 11pt until you change the style. Calibri is a sans-serif font, which means it has no 'tails' on the ends of the strokes of each character. It is used in Excel because it is better suited to numbers and is more legible at larger font sizes. Serif

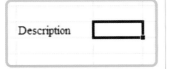

fonts, such as Times New Roman (shown above), are more suitable for use in long segments of small sized text and are used typically in word processor documents.

Watch out

If you combine too many fonts and colours on one spreadsheet it can become illegible and confusing. Stick to one or two fonts of no more than two sizes, make sure that your use of colours does not make the data illegible when it's printed, and use bold formatting judiciously.

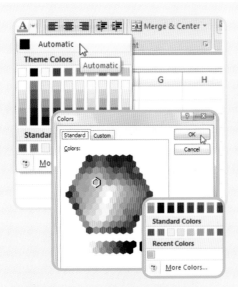

4 To revert to black data, click on **Automatic** at the top of the Font Color palette. If a colour you want is not on the palette, click on **More Colors**. Click on the **Standard** tab and select a new colour from the hexagonal palette and click on **OK** twice. Your new colour will now be displayed under 'Recent Colors'.

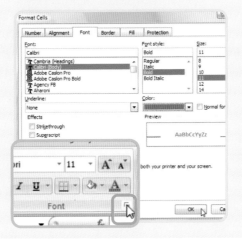

5 If you want to make several changes – font size, style and colour – to a selected range of cells all in one go, you can do this using the Format Cells dialogue box. Click on the dialogue box launcher at the bottom right of the 'Font' group. The Font tab gives a wide range of style options and font effects. The 'Preview' pane displays how your changes will affect the selected cells once you click on **OK**.

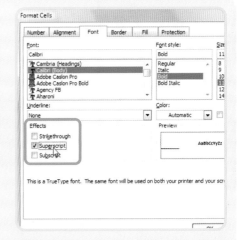

6 There are a few advanced data-formatting options available in the 'Effects' section under the Font tab. Strikethrough can be used to indicate data that is redundant but that you do not want to delete, for example, '~~Overdue~~'. Superscript positions text, such as 'th' or 'rd', above the line – as in '4th' and '3rd'. Subscript is used for text you want to position below the line, such as the '2' in 'H_2O'.

Aligning data

By default, Excel positions numbers to the right of cells and text to the left. However, you can position your data any way you like – for instance, the heading above a column of figures can look better if it is aligned to the right. Excel has a number of alignment options that you can use to style your spreadsheet and make your data more comprehensible.

SEE ALSO...
● *Columns and rows p106*
● *Format your data p108*

BEFORE YOU START
Create a spreadsheet similar to the one used in the 'Style your data' project (page 110). Note how Excel aligns the text to the left and the numbers to the right of a cell.

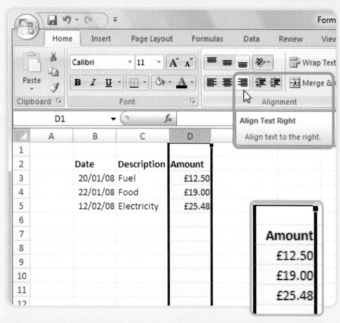

1 Use the **Left**, **Center** and **Right align** buttons in the 'Alignment' group to quickly align text in a selected range of cells. Click on the header of a column that contains both numbers and text, and click on the **Align Text Right** button. Repeat for any other columns that contain a mixture of text and figures.

2 Click on the **Format** button in the 'Cells' group, then on **Format Cells**. In the Format Cells dialogue box, select the **Alignment** tab. You can indent text or change the alignment of data in rows (see Vertical alignment box, above right) and, under 'Orientation', there is an option to display your data at an angle.

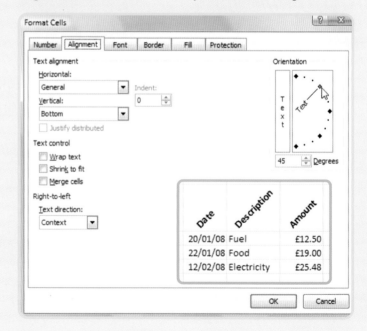

112

Vertical alignment

If you use the 'Wrap text' option – see Step 3 – you should align the data to the top of the cells. This makes it easier to read the row. Highlight all the rows that will contain the wrapped data, excluding any column headings. Open the Format Cells dialogue box and, under the Alignment tab, choose **Top** from the 'Vertical' list box.

Vertical:	
Top	iption
	20/01/08 Fuel
	22/01/08 Food
	12/02/08 Electricity
	(includes
	£5.50
	carried
	forward
	from last
	month)

Watch out

Although text can be centred or aligned anywhere in a cell, numbers should always be aligned to the right, otherwise they become difficult to read. This is because the numbers will not line up correctly in a column of figures.

3 If you have entered more data into a cell than will fit across its width, select the cell and open the Format Cells dialogue box again. Click on the **Alignment** tab and tick the 'Wrap text' option under 'Text control'. This forces Excel to expand the cell downwards so that all the data is visible – see page 104 for information on changing column widths and row heights.

4 You can also merge two cells to create a single cell the size of the two original cells. Just select two or more cells and tick the 'Merge cells' option. In the example below, the cells above 'IN' and 'OUT' need to be merged to provide enough space for the headings, which also need to be centred. You can click on the **Merge & Center** button in the 'Alignment' group as a shortcut to merge cells. This will automatically apply the center alignment to the merged cells.

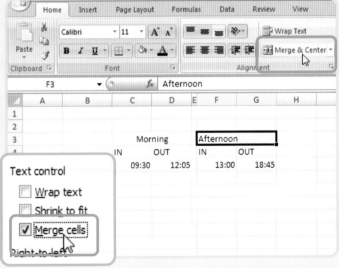

Colours and patterns

Excel includes a range of useful tools to add shades and patterns to cells. Colouring sections of a spreadsheet draws the reader's attention to important figures, and makes it easier to enter and read data in multiple columns. When used in conjunction with Excel's data styling features, these tools can enhance your work, both on screen and on the printed page.

SEE ALSO...
● *Using AutoSum* p100
● *Style your data* p110

BEFORE YOU START
Set up a spreadsheet with some sample dates, text and amounts in columns with headings. Add up the amounts using the **AutoSum** function (see page 100).

1 First, click and drag to select the cells that contain the column headings 'Date', 'Description' and 'Amount'. Then click on the downward arrow next to the 'Font Color' button in the 'Font' group and make the text white. Finally, click on the **Bold** button to embolden the text.

2 To the left of the 'Font Color' button is the 'Fill Color' button – it has a bucket icon on it. With the row of data you just formatted still highlighted, click on the downward arrow next to the 'Fill Color' button and click on the black square in the Theme Colors palette. This colours the background of the selected cells black.

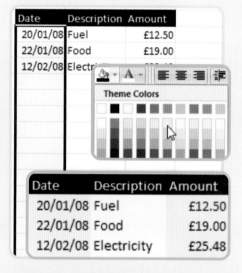

3 Select 50 rows of the 'Date' column (excluding the heading) by clicking in the first cell under the heading and dragging the cursor down the column. Click on the 'Red, Lighter 80%' colour in the Theme Colors palette and leave the font colour as black. Choose different pale backgrounds for the 'Description' and 'Amount' columns.

Watch out
Be careful that the cell colour does not clash with the font colour. If you choose a dark fill, make the data a light colour so it stands out. If you are printing in black and white, coloured data will print as black, and won't show up against a dark fill, so choose white data.

Expert advice
Excel 2007 offers a selection of pre-defined colour sets with backgrounds and foregrounds that are easily distinguishable. These are called 'Theme colours'. When you click on the **Fill** or **Font colour** buttons in the 'Font' group and hover your mouse pointer over a colour in the Theme Colors palette, a pop-up description displays the colour name, theme name and theme group number. If you pick a text and background colour with the same group number, you can be sure they will work well together.

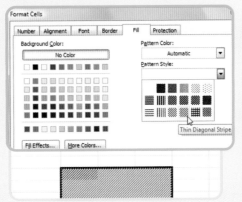

5 If you want to apply a pattern colour and style to a cell, you can use the Format Cells dialogue box. One advantage of this method is that you can see a preview of how the cell will look before clicking on **OK**. Click on the **Format** button, then on **Format Cells**, then click on the **Fill** tab. Use the palettes to select a colour and the drop-down list under 'Pattern Style' to choose a background pattern. Check the results under 'Sample' and when you are happy, click on the **OK** button.

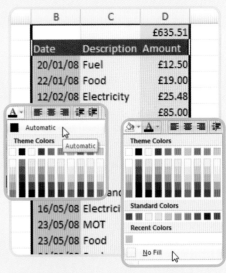

4 Click on the cell containing the AutoSum formula. Click on the **Fill Color** button and make it bright yellow. Now the 'Total' is clearly visible and the eye can easily scan down the columns of data, making it easier to enter and read information.

6 To quickly remove fill and font colours from your spreadsheet, select the range of cells, as above, click on the **Font Color** button and click on **Automatic** at the top of the palette. Then click on the **Fill Color** button and choose **No Fill**. This makes your text black and removes the fill colour from your cells.

Working with page breaks

If you print a large spreadsheet, Excel will automatically split the data into sections according to the size of the paper in your printer. As a result, linked information may be divided over two pages, or headings may be split from related data. But, by using page breaks, you can instruct Excel to print your data the way you want it to be seen.

SEE ALSO...
- *Columns and rows* p104
- *Print your work* p121

BEFORE YOU START
*Open your loan calculator (page 56). Click on the **Page Layout** tab,* *then on the Page Setup dialogue box launcher. Check 'A4 paper' is selected and 'Scaling' is 100%.*

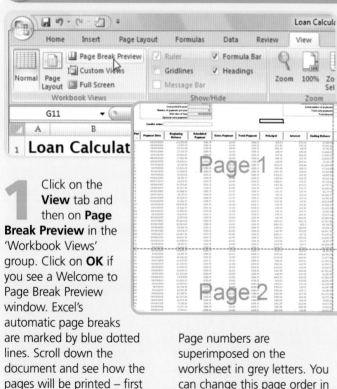

1 Click on the **View** tab and then on **Page Break Preview** in the 'Workbook Views' group. Click on **OK** if you see a Welcome to Page Break Preview window. Excel's automatic page breaks are marked by blue dotted lines. Scroll down the document and see how the pages will be printed – first down your sheet, then across one column and down again.

Page numbers are superimposed on the worksheet in grey letters. You can change this page order in the Page Setup dialogue box to 'Over, then down'.

2 In this example, the last column of data – 'Cumulative Interest' – is overflowing onto pages three and four. Click the vertical blue dotted line and drag it to the right to include all your columns. You can move the horizontal breaks too. This drag and drop method of moving page breaks works well for spreadsheets with only two or three pages but for larger spreadsheets you should insert manual page breaks.

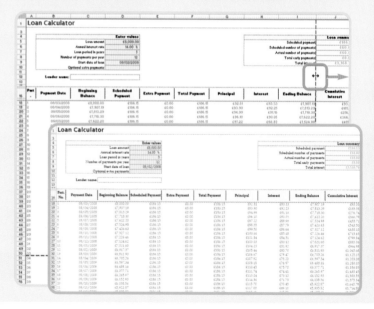

Expert advice
If you have created a large spreadsheet, you can set up your column headings to print on every page so it is easier to read the multiple pages of data. Select the **Sheet** tab in the Page Setup dialogue box and, under 'Print Titles', click on the **Collapse Dialogue** button. Then select the columns you want to be repeated. Click on the button again to open the dialogue box and then click on **OK**. The loan template is set up to print column headings on each page automatically.

Watch out
When you move any page break down or to the right in the Page Break Preview window, Excel reduces the scaling of each page to make the pages fit. To reset the page size, click on the **Page Layout** tab, and then on the Page Setup dialogue box launcher. Then select the **Page** tab and type '100' next to 'Adjust to'.

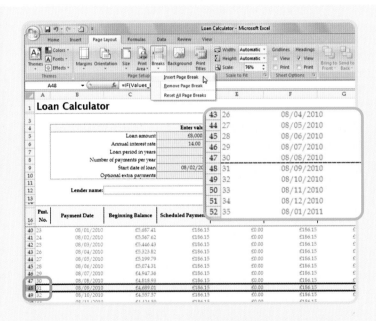

3 To split your data at a specific point you can insert page breaks manually. Click on the **View** tab, then on **Normal** in the 'Workbook Views' group. Click on the row number above which you want to insert a break, select the **Page Layout** tab, then **Breaks**, and then **Insert Page Break**. A dotted line appears above the row. You can also insert page breaks before columns in this way.

4 If you insert or delete columns or rows (see page 104), check the Page Break Preview window regularly to make sure your data is going to print correctly. If necessary, you can drag the page breaks to correct any problems. If you have accidentally inserted two page breaks close together, drag the one you want to remove on top of the other to delete it. To reset all your page breaks, right-click on any cell in Page Break Preview and select **Reset All Page Breaks**.

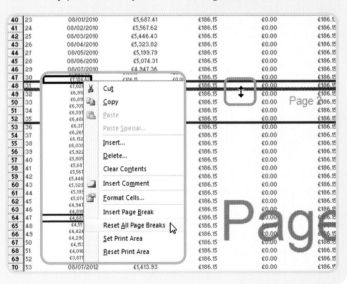

Sort your data

Whether you are using a spreadsheet to store a list of items or to calculate your monthly expenditure, it is useful to organise the information with the dates in order and any names or descriptions alphabetically listed. To save time and effort, Excel has a powerful sort feature, which carefully rearranges your data in ascending or descending order.

BEFORE YOU START
Set up a spreadsheet listing details of your friends and relatives under the headings, 'Last name', 'First name' and 'Birthday'. Add a border under the headings.

1 To sort your new database of birthdays by date, click anywhere in the column of dates to select a single cell. Click on the **Sort & Filter** button in the 'Editing' group on the Home tab, and then on **Sort Oldest to Newest**. You can reverse this sort by clicking on the **Undo** button on the Quick Access Toolbar.

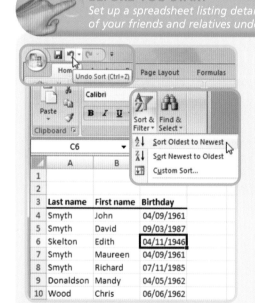

2 To sort your data with the most recent date at the top of the list, click on the **Sort & Filter** button in the 'Editing' group, and then on **Sort Newest to Oldest**. As before, you can reverse this by clicking on the **Undo** button on the Quick Access Toolbar.

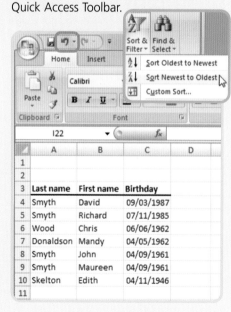

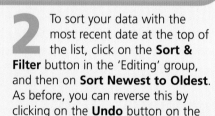

3 Excel automatically assumes that the column in which you initially clicked is the one you want to use for the sort. By selecting **Custom Sort** from the 'Sort & Filter' options, you can select any of your columns. In the Sort dialogue box select **Last name** from the 'Sort by' drop-down list under 'Column' and **A to Z** from the 'Order' list. Make sure 'My data has headers' is selected, and click on **OK**. Your list is now sorted alphabetically by last name. You can do the same by first name.

Watch out
If you have applied formatting, such as borders and cell colours, to your list you will find they are moved with the data when you perform the sort. Keep fills and borders in your lists simple and avoid row gaps because Excel will put them at the bottom of the list when it sorts.

Expert advice
If the data you want to sort has no column headings, or the headings are not directly above the rows you want to sort, de-select the 'My data has headers' option in the Sort dialogue box. You can then select the letter of the column by which you want to sort from the 'Sort by' drop-down list under 'Column'.

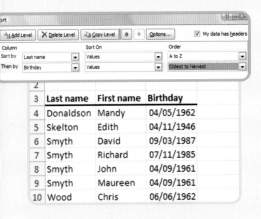

5 Your list will now be sorted by last name first and then by birthday. This means any people who share a surname will be listed first in alphabetical order and then by their birthday. If your list contained people who shared the same birthday and surname, you could sort your list by a third criteria, so that people are sorted by surname alphabetically, then birthday, then first name alphabetically.

4 If your list contains family members who share the same surname, you can sort your list by two criteria. For example, you could sort by last name and then by birthday. Click anywhere in your list and then on **Sort & Filter**, then **Custom Sort**. In the Sort dialogue box, select **Last name** from the 'Sort by' box under 'Column'. Click on the **Add Level** button and select **Birthday** in the 'Then by' box. Select the **Oldest to Newest** option under 'Order' and click on **OK**.

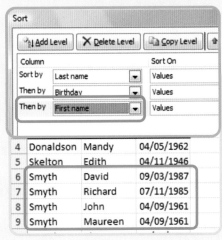

6 If your data contains the names of months, you can instruct Excel to sort them in month order instead of alphabetically. Click in the 'Month' column, open the Sort dialogue box and select **Custom List** in the drop-down list under 'Order'. Under 'Custom lists', choose the list that matches your data and click on **OK**. Make sure **Month** is selected in the 'Sort by' box under 'Column' and click on **OK** again.

Insert a comment

Aspreadsheet may contain data or formulas that the user may not understand, but it is not always convenient to type notes directly on to the sheet. However, you can add pop-up comments to any cell. Each cell with an attached comment has a small red triangle in the top-right corner – the comment only appears while the mouse pointer is hovering over the cell.

SEE ALSO...
● *Explore the program* p16
● *Cut, copy and paste* p102

WORKING WITH COMMENTS

Open a file you have created already, or set up a new one containing some sample data.

Add a comment

To insert a comment, first select the cell to which you want to attach the comment, then click on the **Review** tab and then on **New Comment** in the 'Comments' group. A small window pops up, into which you can enter some explanatory text. Click away from the comment when you have finished typing. A red triangle is displayed in the top right of the cell indicating there is a comment attached.

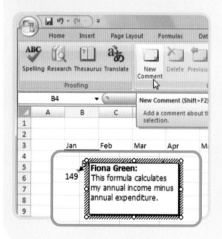

Read a comment

Now, move the mouse pointer over the cell. The comment pops up and remains visible while the pointer is over the cell. To edit the comment, first select the cell, then click on the **Review**

tab and choose **Edit Comment** in the 'Comments' group. To remove a comment, select the cell, click on the **Review** tab and click on **Delete**. As a shortcut, you can right-click the cell and choose **Edit Comment** or **Delete Comment** from the pop-up menu.

Viewing all comments

If you want to see all the comments on your spreadsheet, click on the **Review** tab and click on **Show All Comments** in the 'Comments' group. All your comments will be displayed next to their cells. You can click and drag them around by their edges if one comment is obscuring another. Click on the 'Previous' and 'Next' arrow buttons to move through the spreadsheet one comment at a time forwards or backwards.

Clicking on the **Show/Hide Comment** button will hide a comment if it is displayed and show a comment if it is hidden.

Printing comments

You can print your comments, either as they appear on the spreadsheet when you view them, or all together at the bottom of the last printed page.

Click on the **Page Layout** tab and click on the Page Setup dialogue box launcher. Then click on the **Sheet** tab and choose 'As

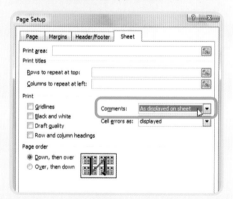

displayed on sheet' in the 'Comments' box to print your comments where they appear, or choose 'At end of sheet' if you don't want your data to be obscured by the comment boxes.

Print your work

Excel's vast horizontal and vertical grid of cells means that it is usually not possible to print your data properly without first defining the area you want to print and then telling the program how to lay out the page. Fortunately, there's a Print Preview window and lots of built-in tools to assist you in fitting your data to the selected paper size.

SEE ALSO...

● *Working with page breaks* p116

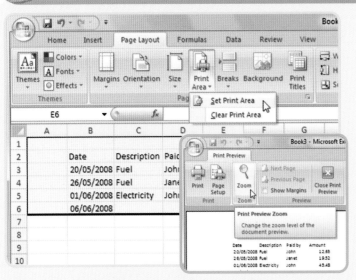

1 Click on the **Page Layout** tab, then on **Print Area** in the 'Page Setup' group and choose **Set Print Area**. Click on the **Office** button and then on **Print Preview** to see how your selected range will look when printed. Click on the **Zoom** button to see a close-up. If there are more pages to view, either below the currently visible page or to the right of it, click the **Next Page** button to see them – by default, the pages are displayed down first, then across (see page 116).

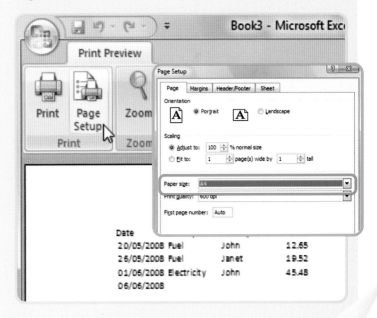

2 Click the **Page Setup** button to open the Page Setup dialogue box, which you can use to change the way your selected range will print. Click on the **Page** tab and first make sure that the correct size for the paper in your printer is selected in the drop-down list next to 'Paper size' – this is usually A4. If you are printing to a different paper size, select it from the list.

Key word

A radio button is a small circle next to an option in a dialogue box. To select the option, click once on the circle or its accompanying text, and a dot will appear. Clicking again deselects the option.

Quick printing

To print a selected area of your spreadsheet quickly, highlight the range of cells you want to print by clicking and dragging. Then click on the **Office** button and choose **Print**. Choose the 'Selection' option under 'Print what' and click the **Preview** button. Check the selection is going to print correctly and click on the **Print** button.

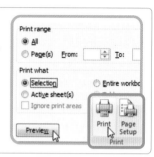

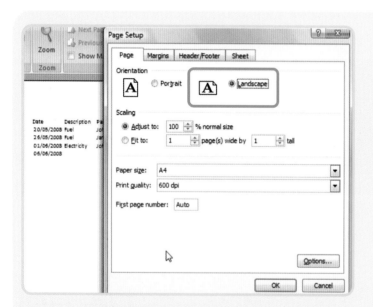

4 Excel includes a useful tool that automatically fits the selected data to the width and height of a fixed number of pages. If most of your data fits the width of the page in the Print Preview window, click on **Page Setup**, select 'Fit to' under 'Scaling' and select '1' next to 'page(s) wide by'. Similarly, if your data almost fits the vertical page, select '1' next to 'tall'. It may be necessary to experiment with the settings to get the right layout. For instance, your data might be printed too small if you choose one page wide for a very wide print area. To restore your data to full size, put a dot next to 'Adjust to' and enter or choose '100' in the box to the left of '% normal size'.

3 If your data is laid out using a lot of columns, click on 'Landscape' to add a dot in the **radio button** next to this option in the 'Orientation' section – this prints the page with the longest side running across so more columns can be fitted onto one page. Click on the **OK** button to return to 'Print Preview' mode and see how your changes have affected the page. Click on the **Page Setup** button again to make further changes.

The Print Manager

If you change your mind after pressing the **Print** button, you can cancel the command as long as the printer hasn't started the job. A printer icon will appear in the System Tray on your Desktop. Double-click on this and select the page you have just sent to the printer. Click on the **Document** menu and select **Cancel**. Note that some printers have their own software – consult the printer manufacturer's manual for details.

Close up

Sometimes a large spreadsheet will not fit the page correctly. When this happens, you must insert page breaks to make sure your data prints properly. For more information, see 'Working with page breaks', page 116.

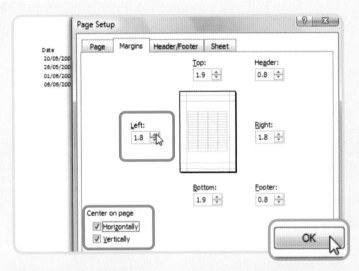

6 Once you are happy with your print preview, click on the **Print** button. This opens the Print dialogue box, where you can choose a range of pages and select the number of copies to print. Click on the **OK** button when you have selected the options. You are returned to the normal view window and your page prints.

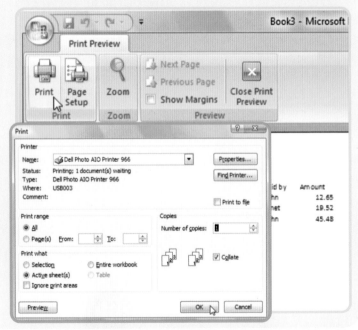

5 If you want your print area to be aligned in the middle of the page, click on the **Page Setup** button in the **Print Preview** tab. Then select the **Margins** tab and put ticks next to 'Horizontally' and 'Vertically' under 'Center on page' – the small preview pane shows how this will affect your printout. If you intend to bind your printouts to make a booklet, widen the left margin by clicking the up arrow in the 'Left' box – your data will be centred between the new margins. Then click on the **OK** button to return to the **Print Preview** window.

How to do just about anything
Computer Essentials

is based on material in *How to do just about anything in Microsoft® Windows® Vista™*, *How to do just about anything in Microsoft® Word 2007* and *How to do just about anything in Microsoft® Excel 2007*, all published by The Reader's Digest Association Limited, London.

First edition copyright © 2008
The Reader's Digest Association Limited,
11 Westferry Circus, Canary Wharf, London E14 4HE.
www.readersdigest.co.uk

We are committed both to the quality of our products and the service we provide to our customers. We value your comments, so please do contact us on **08705 113366**, or via our Web site at **www.readersdigest.co.uk**
If you have any comments or suggestions about this book, e-mail us at **gbeditorial@readersdigest.co.uk**

Origination: Colour Systems Limited, London

Printed and bound in China

Editor
Rachel Weaver

Art Editor
Conorde Clarke

Designer
Wai Sing Tang

Index
Marie Lorimer

Reader's Digest General Books

Editorial Director
Julian Browne

Art Director
Anne-Marie Bulat

Head of Book Development
Sarah Bloxham

Managing Editor
Nina Hathway

Picture Resource Manager
Sarah Stewart-Richardson

Pre-press Account Manager
Dean Russell

Production Controller
Sandra Fuller

Acknowledgments
Dell Computer Corporation
Microsoft Press Office
Symantec

Book code 400-416 UP0000-1
ISBN 978 0 276 44210 0
Oracle code 250013136H.00.24